Lecture Notes
in Economics and
Mathematical Systems

Managing Editors: M. Beckmann and W. Krelle

280

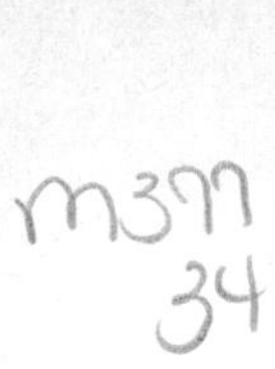

H. T. Lau

Combinatorial Heuristic Algorithms with FORTRAN

Springer-Verlag
Berlin Heidelberg New York London Paris Tokyo

Managing Editors

Prof. Dr. M. Beckmann
Brown University
Providence, RI 02912, USA

Prof. Dr. W. Krelle
Institut für Gesellschafts- und Wirtschaftswissenschaften
der Universität Bonn
Adenauerallee 24–42, D-5300 Bonn, FRG

Author

Dr. H.T. Lau
Bell-Northern Research
3, Place du Commerce
Verdun, Quebec
Canada, H3E 1H6

ISBN 3-540-17161-4 Springer-Verlag Berlin Heidelberg New York
ISBN 0-387-17161-4 Springer-Verlag New York Berlin Heidelberg

Library of Congress Cataloging-in-Pubication Data. Lau, H.T. (Hang Tong), 1952- Combinatorial heuristic algorithms with FORTRAN. (Lecture notes in economics and mathematical systems; 280) Bibliography: p. 1. Combinatorial optimization–Data processing. 2. Algorithms. 3. FORTRAN (Computer program language) I. Title. II. Series.
QA402.5.L37 1986 511'.8 86-26103
ISBN 0-387-17161-4 (U.S.)

Printed in Germany

Printing and binding: Druckhaus Beltz, Hemsbach/Bergstr.
2142/3140-543210

Lecture Notes in Economics and Mathematical Systems

Managing Editors: M. Beckmann and W. Krelle

280

H. T. Lau

Combinatorial Heuristic Algorithms with FORTRAN

Springer-Verlag

Berlin Heidelberg New York London Paris Tokyo

Author

Dr. H. T. Lau
Bell-Northern Research
3, Place du Commerce
Verdun, Quebec
Canada, H3E 1H6

ISBN 3-540-17161-4 Springer-Verlag Berlin Heidelberg New York
ISBN 0-387-17161-4 Springer-Verlag New York Berlin Heidelberg

Library of Congress Cataloging-in-Pubication Data. Lau, H. T. (Hang Tong), 1952- Combinatorial heuristic algorithms with FORTRAN. (Lecture notes in economics and mathematical systems; 280) Bibliography: p. 1. Combinatorial optimization–Data processing. 2. Algorithms. 3. FORTRAN (Computer program language) I. Title. II. Series.
QA402.5.L37 1986 511'.8 86-26103
ISBN 0-387-17161-4 (U.S.)

Printed in Germany

Printing and binding: Druckhaus Beltz, Hemsbach/Bergstr.
2142/3140-543210

PREFACE

In recent years researchers have spent much effort in developing efficient heuristic algorithms for solving the class of NP-complete problems which are widely believed to be inherently intractable from the computational point of view. Although algorithms have been designed and are notorious among researchers, computer programs are either not implemented on computers or very difficult to obtain. The purpose of this book is to provide a source of FORTRAN coded algorithms for a selected number of well-known combinatorial optimization problems. The book is intended to be used as a supplementary text in combinatorial algorithms, network optimization, operations research and management science. In addition, a short description on each algorithm will allow the book to be used as a convenient reference.

This work would not have been possible without the excellent facilities of Bell-Northern Research, Canada.

H. T. Lau

Ile des Soeurs
Quebec, Canada

August 1986

CONTENTS

INTRODUCTION

Following the elegant theory of NP-completeness, the idea of developing efficient heuristic algorithms has been gaining its popularity and significance. Combinatorial graph algorithms and network design problems are among the areas receiving the most attention. It would be very difficult to give a complete coverage of the combinatorial heuristic algorithms. The eight topics in this book are selected from the areas of integer programming and network design. While the choice of the problems and algorithms reflects the author's interest, they are all widely known. In particular, the problem in each chapter has been shown to be NP-complete.

The same format has been used for each chapter which is largely independent and self-contained. Following the discussion of the problem and algorithm, a detail description of the parameters of the subroutine is given. Then a small test example will illustrate the usage of the subroutine. The program listings are printed directly from the computer to minimize the typing errors. All computer programs in this book are written in FORTRAN 77, and test runs were performed on the Amdahl 5870 using the IBM VS FORTRAN Compiler.

For background material on graph theory, linear programming, network optimization and NP-complete theory, the reader is referred to standard works such as :

Graph Theory with Applications, J. A. Bondy, U.S.R. Murty, The Macmillan Press, 1976.

Linear Programming, V. Chvátal, W.H. Freeman & Co., 1983.

Combinatorial Optimization: Networks and Matroids, E. L. Lawler, Holt, Rinehart and Winston, 1976.

Computers and Intractability: A Guide to the Theory of NP-completeness, M. R. Garey, D. S. Johnson, W. H. Freeman & Co., 1979.

Chapter 1

INTEGER LINEAR PROGRAMMING

A. Problem Description

The *integer linear programming problem* has the form

$$\text{maximize} \quad \sum_{j=1}^{n} c_j x_j$$

$$\text{subject to} \quad \sum_{j=1}^{n} a_{ij} x_j \le b_i \qquad (i=1,2,\ldots,m)$$

$$x_j > 0 \qquad (j=1,2,\ldots,n)$$

$$x_j \text{ is an integer} \qquad (j=1,2,\ldots,n)$$

such that c_j, a_{ij} and b_i are real numbers.

The heuristic procedure to be described will find a vector x which is feasible and gives a reasonably good objective function value. In general, it is very hard even to decide whether a given integer linear programming problem has a feasible solution. Thus it is not surprising that the heuristic procedure sometimes fails to deliver a feasible solution even if there is one. This might happen when dealing with tightly constrained problems.

B. Algorithm

Step 1. Use the simplex method to find an optimal solution

$$z = (z_1, z_2, \ldots, z_n)$$

of the integer linear programming problem with the integrality constraint removed.

The simplex method will point out a set of nonbasic slack variables P and a set of nonslack basic variables Q, where

$$P \subseteq \{1, 2, \ldots, m\}$$

$$Q \subseteq \{1, 2, \ldots, n\} .$$

More precisely, P and Q are sets such that

(a) for every choice of numbers d_i $(i \in P)$, the system

$$\sum_{j \in Q} a_{ij} x_j = d_i \qquad (i \in P)$$

has a unique solution;

(b) the unique solution of

$$\sum_{j \in Q} a_{ij} x_j = b_i \qquad (i \in P)$$

$$x_j = 0 \qquad (j \notin Q)$$

is an optimal solution of the integer linear programming problem with the integrality constraint removed.

Step 2. Find the unique solution

$$y = (y_1, y_2, \ldots)$$

of the following system

$$\sum_{j \in Q} a_{ij} y_j = b_i - 1/2 \sum_{j \in Q} |a_{ij}| \qquad (i \in P)$$

$$y_j = 0 \qquad (j \notin Q).$$

Step 3. Move from the vector y (found in Step 2) to the vector z (found in Step 1) along the interpolated line segment between y and z, and round off every encountered point to its nearest integer point. This can be achieved by finding all the values of t for which there is a subscript j satisfying

$$y_j + t(z_j - y_j) = \text{integer} + 1/2$$

$$0 < t < 1 .$$

Suppose there are k such values of t. Sort these values into the order of

$$t_1 < t_2 < \ldots < t_k$$

and set $t_0 = 0$ and $t_{k+1} = 1$.

For each $i = 0, 1, \ldots, k$, use a value s such that

$$t_i < s < t_{i+1}$$

and round each

$$y_j + s(z_j - y_j)$$

to the nearest integer x_j.

Thus $k+1$ integer points are obtained; among the feasible ones, choose that which maximizes the objective function

$$\Sigma\, c_j x_j \ .$$

Step 4. Starting from the feasible solution obtained in Step 3, search for better feasible solutions by a two part procedure. The first part consists of successively increasing or decreasing some variable by one as long as each resulting solution is better than the preceding one. The second part is to search for better solutions by changing two variables simultaneously. The two parts of the procedure are applied repeatedly until no better solution is found.

C. Subroutine INTLP Parameters

Input :

M - number of constraints.

N - number of variables.

M1 - equal to M + 1.

NM - equal to N + M.

A - real matrix of dimension M1 by NM+1 containing the coefficients of the constraints in the first M rows, the last row and the last M+1 columns are used as working storages.

B - real vector of length M containing the right hand sides of the constraints.

C - real vector of length N containing the coefficients of the objective function.

IADIM - row dimension of matrix A exactly as specified in the dimension statement of the calling program.

Output :

X - real vector of length max(M1,N) containing the solution.

INFS - integer error indicator;
INFS = 0 indicates that a solution is found,
INFS = 1 indicates that the program is infeasible.

Working Storages :

WK1 - real matrix of dimension N by N;
WK1(i,j) is the ratio C(i)/C(j), used in controlling the pairwise variable interchange for better solution.

WK2 - real matrix of dimension M1 by M1;
the inverse of the optimal basis.

WK3 - real vector of length N;
permutation of coefficients in the objective function.

WK4 - real vector of length N;
WK4(i) indicates the change in the value of X(i).

WK5 - real vector of length N;
WK5(i) is equal to 1 if C(i) is positive, and -1 if C(i) is negative.

WK6 - real vector of length N;
WK6(i) is a linear combination of two points WK7(i) and WK8(i).

WK7 - real vector of length N;
solution of the linear programming problem without integer constraints.

WK8 - real vector of length N;
solution refined from WK7.

WK9 - real vector of length M;
a measure of the degree of infeasibility of an infeasible solution.

WK10 - real vector of length M;
feasibility test slacks.

WK11 - real vector of length M;
feasibility test slacks, updated from WK10.

WK12 - real vector of length M;
transformed right-hand side of the equations in which the variables can be rounded without violating the constraints.

WK13 - real vector of length M1;
primal prices, used in the simplex subroutine.

WK14 - real vector of length M1;
pivot column, used in the simplex subroutine.

WK15 - real vector of length M1;
a copy of the solution before an improvement attempt.

WK16 - real vector of length max(M1,N);
the new value of WK9 when there is a change in X.

WK17 - boolean vector of length N;
WK17(i) indicates whether WK16(i) is less than WK9(i).

IWK18 - integer vector of length N;
permutation of integers from 1 to N.

IWK19 - integer vector of length M1;
IWK(J+1) is the Jth basic variable, used in the simplex subroutine.

IWK20 - integer vector of length NM;
an initial feasible solution.

D. Test Example

$$\begin{array}{lrcl}
\text{maximize} & -2x_1 + x_2 + 4x_3 - x_4 - 3x_5 & & \\
\text{subject to} & -3x_1 - x_2 + 2x_3 + 3x_4 - 3x_5 & \leq & 1 \\
& x_2 - x_3 - 4x_4 - 2x_5 & \leq & -1 \\
& x_1 + 4x_3 + 3x_4 & \leq & 4 \\
& x_1, x_2, x_3, x_4, x_5 & \geq & 0
\end{array}$$

x_1, x_2, x_3, x_4, x_5 are integers.

Main Program

```
      REAL    A(4,9),B(3),C(5),X(5),WK1(5,5),
     +        WK2(4,4),WK3(5),WK4(5),WK5(5),WK6(5),
     +        WK7(5),WK8(5),WK9(3),WK10(3),WK11(3),
     +        WK12(3),WK13(4),WK14(4),WK15(4),WK16(5)
      LOGICAL WK17(5)
      INTEGER IWK18(5),IWK19(4),IWK20(8)
C
      READ(*,10) M,N
 10   FORMAT(2I5)
      DO 20 I = 1 , M
 20      READ(*,30) (A(I,J),J=1,N)
      READ(*,30) (B(I),I=1,M)
      READ(*,30) (C(I),I=1,N)
 30   FORMAT(5F5.0)
C
      IADIM = 4
      M1 = M + 1
      NM = N + M
      CALL INTLP (M,N,M1,NM,A,B,C,IADIM,X,INFS,
     +           WK1,WK2,WK3,WK4,WK5,WK6,WK7,WK8,WK9,WK10,WK11,
     +           WK12,WK13,WK14,WK15,WK16,WK17,IWK18,IWK19,IWK20)
C
      IF (INFS .EQ. 1) THEN
         WRITE(*,40)
 40      FORMAT(/' THE PROBLEM IS INFEASIBLE '/)
      ELSE
         WRITE(*,50)
 50      FORMAT(/' SOLUTION FOUND :'/)
         WRITE(*,60) (X(I),I=1,N)
 60      FORMAT(1X,5F8.1)
      ENDIF
      STOP
      END
```

Input Data

```
    3    5
-3.  -1.   2.   3.  -3.
 0.   1.  -1.  -4.  -2.
 1.   0.   4.   3.   0.
 1.  -1.   4.
-2.   1.   4.  -1.  -3.
```

Output Results

```
 SOLUTION FOUND :

     0.0     2.0     1.0     0.0     1.0
```

```
      SUBROUTINE INTLP (M,N,M1,NM,A,B,C,IADIM,X,INFS,
     +                  WK1,WK2,WK3,WK4,WK5,WK6,WK7,WK8,WK9,
     +                  WK10,WK11,WK12,WK13,WK14,WK15,WK16,
     +                  WK17,IWK18,IWK19,IWK20)
C
C     Integer linear programming heuristic
C
      REAL    A(IADIM,1),B(M),C(N),X(1),WK1(N,N),WK2(M1,M1),WK3(N),
     +        WK4(N),WK5(N),WK6(N),WK7(N),WK8(N),WK9(M),WK10(M),
     +        WK11(M),WK12(M),WK13(M1),WK14(M1),WK15(M1),WK16(1)
      LOGICAL WK17(N)
      INTEGER IWK18(N),IWK19(M1),IWK20(NM)
      COMMON  /C1/ J,K
      COMMON  /C2/ INIT
C
C     compute the machine epsilon
C
      EPS = 1.0
 10   EPS = EPS / 2.0
         TOL = 1.0 + EPS
         IF (TOL .GT. 1.0)  GO TO 10
      EPS = SQRT(EPS)
C
C     compute the machine infinity
C
      BIG = 1.0E6
 20   BIG = BIG * BIG
         TOL = 1.0 + BIG
         IF (TOL .GT. BIG)  GO TO 20
      BIG = BIG * BIG
C
C     normalize coefficients of the problem
C
      DO 50 I = 1, M
         SUM = 0.0
         DO 30 J = 1, N
 30         SUM = SUM + A(I,J) * A(I,J)
         SUM = SQRT(SUM)
         DO 40 J = 1, N
 40         A(I,J) = A(I,J) / SUM
         B(I) = B(I) / SUM
 50   CONTINUE
      N1 = N + 1
C
C     set up the data for the simplex subroutine
C
      DO 70 I = 1, M
         I1 = M - I + 1
         I2 = M - I + 2
         WK16(I+1) = B(I)
         DO 60 J = 1, N
 60         A(I2,J) = A(I1,J)
 70   CONTINUE
      WK16(1) = 0.
      DO 80 J = 1, N
 80      A(1,J) = -C(J)
      DO 90 J = N1, NM
 90      A(1,J) = 0.
      DO 110 I = 2, M1
         DO 100 J = N1, NM
            A(I,J) = 0.
 100     CONTINUE
 110  CONTINUE
```

```
      DO 120 I = 2, M1
         J = N + I - 1
         A(I,J) = 1.0
 120  CONTINUE
C
C     use the simplex method to find an optimal noninteger solution
C
      CALL SIMPLX(N,M,A,X,INFS,BIG,EPS,
     +            WK2,WK13,WK14,WK16,IWK19,IWK20)
C
      IF (INFS .NE. 0) RETURN
C
C     restore the matrix A to original form
C
      DO 140 I = 1, M
         I1 = I + 1
         DO 130 J = 1, N
 130        A(I,J) = A(I1,J)
 140  CONTINUE
      DO 150 I = 1, M1
 150     WK15(I) = X(I)
      DO 160 J = 1, N
         ISUB = IWK20(J)
         IF (ISUB .GT. 0)  THEN
            WK7(J) = X(ISUB)
         ELSE
            WK7(J) = 0.
         ENDIF
 160  CONTINUE
      JJ = 1
      II = 0
      DO 180 J = 1, M1
         DO 170 I = 1, M1
            II = II + 1
            IF (II .GT. M1)  THEN
               II = 1
               JJ = JJ + 1
            ENDIF
            A(I,N+J) = WK2(II,JJ)
 170     CONTINUE
 180  CONTINUE
      DO 200 I = 1, M
         DO 190 J = 1, M
 190        WK2(I,J) = A(I+1,N+J+1)
 200  CONTINUE
C
C     select a second solution corresponding to the noninteger
C     optimal solution by tightening the binding constraints
C     sufficiently so that a rounded solution still satisfies
C     the original constraints
C
      DO 220 I = 1, M
         ISUB = IWK20(N+I)
         IF (ISUB .GT. 0)  THEN
            IF (X(ISUB) .GT. 0.0)  THEN
               WK12(I) = B(I)
               GOTO 220
            ENDIF
         ENDIF
         TEMP = 0.0
         DO 210 J = 1, N
            IF (IWK20(J) .GT. 0)  TEMP = TEMP + ABS(A(I,J))
 210     CONTINUE
```

```
         WK12(I) = B(I) - 0.5 * TEMP
  220  CONTINUE
C
C      the second solution is stored in WK8
C
       DO 230 J = 1, N
  230     WK8(J) = 0.
       DO 250 I = 1, M
          ISUB = IWK19(I+1)
          IF (ISUB .LE. N)  THEN
             TEMP = 0.
             DO 240 K = 1, M
  240           TEMP = TEMP + WK2(I,K) * WK12(K)
             WK8(ISUB) = TEMP
          ENDIF
  250  CONTINUE
C
C      perform the linear search along the line joined by two points
C      WK7 and WK8 found above
C
       CALL PARSE1(N,M,IADIM,A,B,X,BIG,
     +             WK4,WK6,WK7,WK8,WK9,WK16,WK17)
C
C      search for better feasible solutions
C
       CALL PARSE2(N,M,IADIM,A,B,C,X,WK3,WK5,WK10,IWK18)
C
C      prepare for the interchange of two variables
C
       IF (INIT .GT. 1)  CALL PARSE4(N,C,WK1,IWK18)
C
C      increase or decrease one variable by one as long as the
C      resulting better solution is feasible
C
  260  CALL PARSE3(N,M,IADIM,A,C,X,BIG,WK10)
C
       IF (INIT .LE. 1)  RETURN
       DO 270 J = 1, N
  270     WK6(J) = X(J)
       J = 1
       K = N
C
C      check whether the changed value of a variable is negative
C
  280  CALL PARSE5(M,IADIM,A,X,WK5,WK10,WK11,IWK18,MOVEON)
C
       IF (MOVEON .NE. 1)  THEN
          K = J + 1
          GOTO 320
       ENDIF
  290  ISUB = IWK18(K)
       LL1 = 0
       LL2 = 0
       DO 300 I = 1, M
          IF (WK11(I) .LT. 0.0)  THEN
             IF (A(I,ISUB) .EQ. 0.0)  GOTO 310
             IF (A(I,ISUB) .LT. 0.0)  THEN
                LL1 = 1
             ELSE
                LL2 = 2
             ENDIF
          ENDIF
  300  CONTINUE
```

```
      LL3 = LL1 + LL2
C
C     investigate the possibility of changing X(J) in one favorable
C     direction and seek for a change in another variable X(K)
C
      IF (LL3 .EQ. 2)  THEN
C
C        try to decrease X(K) to get a better solution
C
         CALL PARSE6(N,M,IADIM,A,C,X,BIG,
     +               WK1,WK3,WK5,WK10,WK11,IWK18,MORE)
         IF (MORE .EQ. 1) GOTO 280
      ELSE
         IF (LL3 .LT. 2)  THEN
C
C           try to increase X(K) to get a better solution
C
            CALL PARSE7(N,M,IADIM,A,C,X,BIG,
     +                  WK1,WK3,WK5,WK10,WK11,IWK18,MORE)
            IF (MORE .EQ. 1) GOTO 280
         ENDIF
      ENDIF
 310  IF (J .NE. (K-1))  THEN
         K = K - 1
         GOTO 290
      ENDIF
C
C     consider changing X(J) by one in the other direction and
C     make a small integer change of X(K)
C
C
 320  CALL PARSE8(N,M,IADIM,A,X,WK1,WK5,WK10,WK11,IWK18)
C
      N1 = N - 1
      IF (INIT .LT. N1)  N1 = INIT
C
C     if one or more improved solution is found then
C        repeat the search
C
      IF (J .NE. N1)  THEN
         J = J + 1
         K = N
         GOTO 280
      ENDIF
      DO 330 I = 1, N
         IF (X(I) .NE. WK6(I)) GOTO 260
 330  CONTINUE
C
      RETURN
      END
```

```
      SUBROUTINE SIMPLX (NUMVAR,NUMCON,A,X,INFS,BIG,EPS,
     +                   WK2,WK13,WK14,WK16,IWK19,IWK20)
C
C     This subprogram is used by subroutine INTLP
C
      REAL    A(1),X(1),WK2(1),WK13(1),WK14(1),WK16(1)
      INTEGER IWK19(1),IWK20(1)
C
C     simplex method for linear programming
C
      N = NUMVAR + NUMCON
      IC5 = NUMCON + 1
      M = NUMCON + 1
      IC6 = 2
      IC7 = 1
      MAXITR = 900
      INC1 = 0
      K = 0
      ITER = 0
      INC2 = 0
      IC1 = 0
      JC5 = 0
      DELTA1 = EPS
      DELTA2 = EPS
      DELTA3 = -EPS * 2.
      JC1 = 0
      DELTA4 = 0.
      M2 = M * M
      INFS = 1
      ISPEC = 7777
C
C     start phase one
C
      DO 10 I = 1, M
 10      IWK19(I) = 0
      IC9 = 0
      DO 30 J = 1, N
         IWK20(J) = 0
         IC8 = IC9 + IC6
         LL = IC9 + M
         JC2 = 0
         DO 20 L = IC8, LL
            IF (A(L) .NE. 0.0)  THEN
               JC2 = JC1 + 1
               JC1 = L
            ENDIF
 20      CONTINUE
         IF (JC2 .EQ. 1)  THEN
            JC3 = JC1 - IC9
            IF (IWK19(JC3) .EQ. 0)  THEN
               IF (A(JC1)*WK16(JC3) .GE. 0.0)  THEN
                  IWK19(JC3) = J
                  IWK20(J) = JC3
                  IC9 = IC9 + IC5
               ENDIF
            ENDIF
         ENDIF
 30   CONTINUE
C
C     form the inverse from IWK20
C
 40   LOOP3 = 1
      LOOP2 = 1
```

```
      IF (JC5 .LE. 0)  INC2 = 0
      DO 50 I = 1, M2
 50      WK2(I) = 0.
      IC8 = 1
      DO 60 I = 1, M
         WK2(IC8) = 1.0
         X(I) = WK16(I)
         IC8 = IC8 + M + 1
 60   CONTINUE
      DO 70 I = IC6, M
         IF (IWK19(I) .NE. 0)  IWK19(I) = ISPEC
 70   CONTINUE
      INFS = 1
      IC1 = 1
C
C     form inverse
C
 80   IF (IWK20(IC1)) 250,110,250
C
 90   DELTA5 = 0.
C
C     reset the artificials
C
      DO 100 I = IC6, M
         IF (IWK19(I) .EQ. ISPEC)  THEN
            IF (ABS(WK14(I)) .GT. DELTA5)  THEN
               IC3 = I
               DELTA5 = ABS(WK14(I))
            ENDIF
         ENDIF
 100  CONTINUE
      IF (DELTA5 .LT. DELTA1)  THEN
         IWK20(IC1) = 0
      ELSE
         IWK19(IC3) = IC1
         IWK20(IC1) = IC3
         GOTO 350
      ENDIF
 110  IC1 = IC1 + 1
      IF (IC1 .LE. N) GOTO 80
 120  DO 130 I = 1, M
         IF (IWK19(I) .EQ. ISPEC)  IWK19(I) = 0
 130  CONTINUE
C
      LOOP1 = 1
      LOOP2 = 2
      LOOP3 = 2
C
C     perform one iteration
C
 140  INC3 = 0
      INC4 = 0
      DO 150 I = IC6, M
         IF (ABS(X(I)) .LT. DELTA2)  THEN
            X(I) = 0.
         ELSE
            IF (X(I) .NE. 0.0)  THEN
               IF (X(I) .GT. 0.0)  THEN
                  IF (IWK19(I) .EQ. 0)  INC3 = 1
               ELSE
                  INC4 = 1
                  INC3 = 1
               ENDIF
```

```
            ENDIF
         ENDIF
 150  CONTINUE
C
C     if infeasible then invert again
C
      IF (INFS .LT. INC3)  GOTO 40
      IF (INFS .GT. INC3)  THEN
         INFS = 0
 160     DELTA4 = 0.
      ENDIF
C
C     obtain prices
C
      IC8 = IC7
      DO 170 J = 1, M
         WK13(J) = WK2(IC8)
         IC8 = IC8 + M
 170  CONTINUE
C
C     pricing
C
      IF (INFS .NE. 0)  THEN
         DO 180 J = 1, M
 180        WK13(J) = WK13(J) * DELTA4
         DO 210 I = IC6, M
            IC8 = I
            IF (X(I) .LT. 0.0)  THEN
               DO 190 J = 1, M
                  WK13(J) = WK13(J) + WK2(IC8)
                  IC8 = IC8 + M
 190           CONTINUE
            ELSE
               IF (IWK19(I) .EQ. 0)  THEN
                  DO 200 J = 1, M
                     WK13(J) = WK13(J) - WK2(IC8)
                     IC8 = IC8 + M
 200              CONTINUE
               ENDIF
            ENDIF
 210     CONTINUE
      ENDIF
C
C     select entering column
C
      IC1 = 0
      DELTA7 = DELTA3
      IC2 = 1
 220  IF (IWK20(IC2))  240,460,240
C
 230  IF (DELTA6 .LT. DELTA7)  THEN
         DELTA7 = DELTA6
         IC1 = IC2
      ENDIF
 240  IC2 = IC2 + 1
C
C     all costs are non-negative
C
      IF (IC2 .LE. N)  GOTO 220
      IF (IC1 .LE. 0)  THEN
         K = 3 + INFS
         GOTO 340
```

```
      ENDIF
C
C     multiply the column into the basis inverse
C
 250  DO 260 I = 1, M
 260     WK14(I) = 0.
      IC4 = IC1 * IC5 - IC5
      LL = 0
      DO 280 I = 1, M
         IC4 = IC4 + 1
         IF (A(IC4) .NE. 0.0)  THEN
            DO 270 J = 1, M
               LL = LL + 1
 270           WK14(J) = WK14(J) + A(IC4) * WK2(LL)
         ELSE
            LL = LL + M
         ENDIF
 280  CONTINUE
C
      GOTO (90,290,480), LOOP2
C
C     get the maximum value from the pivot column
C
 290  IC3 = 0
      DELTA8 = 0.
      JC3 = 0
      DO 310 I = IC6, M
         IF (X(I) .EQ. 0.0)  THEN
            BETA = ABS(WK14(I))
            IF (BETA .GT. DELTA1)  THEN
               IF (IWK19(I) .EQ. 0)  GOTO 300
               IF (JC3 .EQ. 0)  THEN
                  IF (WK14(I) .GT. 0.0)  THEN
 300                 IF (JC3 .NE. 0)  THEN
                        IF (BETA .GT. DELTA8)  THEN
                           DELTA8 = BETA
                           IC3 = I
                        ENDIF
                     ELSE
                        JC3 = 1
                        DELTA8 = BETA
                        IC3 = I
                     ENDIF
                  ENDIF
               ENDIF
            ENDIF
         ENDIF
 310  CONTINUE
C
C     find the maximum pivot from the positive equations
C
      IF (IC3 .EQ. 0)  THEN
         DELTA8 = BIG
         DO 320 IT = IC6, M
            IF (WK14(IT) .GT. DELTA1)  THEN
               IF (X(IT) .GT. 0.0)  THEN
                  DELTA9 = X(IT) / WK14(IT)
                  IF (DELTA9 .LT. DELTA8)  THEN
                     DELTA8 = DELTA9
                     IC3 = IT
                  ELSE
                     IF (DELTA9 .EQ. DELTA8)  THEN
                        IF (IWK19(IT) .EQ. 0)  THEN
```

```
                          DELTA8 = DELTA9
                          IC3 = IT
                       ENDIF
                    ENDIF
                 ENDIF
              ENDIF
           ENDIF
  320   CONTINUE
C
C       find pivot among negative equations
C
        IF (INC4 .NE. 0)  THEN
           DELTA7 = -DELTA1
           DO 330 I = IC6, M
              IF (X(I) .LT. 0.0)  THEN
                 IF (WK14(I) .LT. DELTA7)  THEN
                    IF (WK14(I)*DELTA8 .LE. X(I))  THEN
                       DELTA7 = WK14(I)
                       IC3 = I
                    ENDIF
                 ENDIF
              ENDIF
  330      CONTINUE
        ENDIF
     ENDIF
C
C    test pivot
C
     IF (IC3 .LE. 0)  THEN
        K = 5
  340   IF (DELTA4) 160,400,160
     ENDIF
C
C    terminate if too many iterations
C
     IF (ITER .LT. MAXITR)  THEN
  350   BETA = -WK14(IC3)
        WK14(IC3) = -1.
        LL = 0
C
C       transform inverse
C
        DO 370 L = IC3, M2, M
           IF (WK2(L) .EQ. 0.0)  THEN
              LL = LL + M
           ELSE
              DELTA9 = WK2(L) / BETA
              WK2(L) = 0.
              DO 360 I = 1, M
                 LL = LL + 1
  360            WK2(LL) = WK2(LL) + DELTA9 * WK14(I)
           ENDIF
  370   CONTINUE
C
C       transform X
C
        DELTA9 = X(IC3) / BETA
        X(IC3) = 0.
        DO 380 I = 1, M
  380      X(I) = X(I) + DELTA9 * WK14(I)
C
C       restore the pivot
C
```

```
          WK14(IC3) = -BETA
C
          GOTO (120,390), LOOP3
C
 390      JC3 = IWK19(IC3)
          IF (JC3 .GT. 0)  IWK20(JC3) = 0
          IWK20(IC1) = IC3
          IWK19(IC3) = IC1
          JC5 = 0
          ITER = ITER + 1
          INC2 = INC2 + 1
          IF (INC2 - INC1) 140,40,140
       ENDIF
C
       K = 6
C
C      error checking
C
 400   LOOP1 = 2
       DO 410 I = 1, M
 410      WK14(I) = -WK16(I)
       DO 430 I = 1, M
          JC4 = IWK19(I)
          IF (JC4 .NE. 0)  THEN
             JC3 = IC5 * (JC4 - 1)
             DO 420 IT = 1, M
                JC3 = JC3 + 1
                IF (A(JC3) .NE. 0.0) WK14(IT) = WK14(IT) + X(I)*A(JC3)
 420         CONTINUE
          ENDIF
 430   CONTINUE
C
C      set error flags
C
       I = 1
 440   IC2 = IWK19(I)
       IF (IC2 .EQ. 0)  THEN
 450      I = I + 1
          IF (I .LE. M) GOTO 440
          IF (JC5 .EQ. 0)  JC5 = 4
          IF (K .NE. 5)  RETURN
          LOOP2 = 3
          GOTO 250
       ENDIF
 460   DELTA6 = 0.
C
C      price out a column
C
       LL = (IC2 - 1) * IC5
       DO 470 IC8 = 1, M
          LL = LL + 1
          IF (A(LL) .NE. 0.0)  DELTA6 = DELTA6 + WK13(IC8) * A(LL)
 470   CONTINUE
C
       GOTO (230,450), LOOP1
C
 480   RETURN
       END
```

```
      SUBROUTINE PARSE1(N,M,IADIM,A,B,X,BIG,
     +                  WK4,WK6,WK7,WK8,WK9,WK16,WK17)
C
C     This subprogram is used by subroutine INTLP
C
      REAL    A(IADIM,1),B(1),X(1),WK4(1),WK6(1),WK7(1),
     +        WK8(1),WK9(1),WK16(1)
      LOGICAL WK17(1)
C
C     linear search
C
      EPSILN = -BIG
      DELPS = 0.05
      DELTA = 0.
 10   TEMP = 1.0 - DELTA
C
C     form a linear combination of WK7 and WK8
C
      DO 20 J = 1, N
 20      WK6(J) = WK7(J) + DELTA * (WK8(J) - WK7(J))
      DO 30 J = 1, N
         IF (WK6(J) .LE. 0.)  THEN
            X(J) = 0.
         ELSE
            X(J) = AINT(WK6(J) + 0.5)
         ENDIF
 30   CONTINUE
C
C     compute WK9 the degree of infeasibility
C
      DO 50 I = 1, M
         YY1 = 0.
         DO 40 J = 1, N
 40         YY1 = YY1 + A(I,J) * X(J)
 50      WK9(I) = YY1 - B(I)
      XWORK = 0.
      DO 60 I = 1, M
         IF (WK9(I) .GT. 0.0)  XWORK = XWORK + WK9(I)
 60   CONTINUE
 70   IF (XWORK .LE. 0.0)  RETURN
      LL = M
C
C     compute the change in solution X that improves the objective
C     value,  this is indicated by WK4
C
 80   INCR = 0
      XX1 = EPSILN
      KK = 0
      DO 150 J = 1, N
         YY1 = 0.
         YY2 = 0.
         DO 90 I = 1, LL
            IF (WK9(I) .GT. 0.)  YY1 = YY1 + A(I,J)
 90      CONTINUE
         XX2 = ABS(YY1)
         IF (YY1 .LT. 0.)  THEN
            WK4(J) = 1.0
            GOTO 100
         ELSE
            IF (YY1 .GT. 0.)  THEN
               IF (X(J) .GT. 0.0)  THEN
                  WK4(J) = -1.0
                  GOTO 120
```

```
              ENDIF
           ENDIF
        ENDIF
        WK4(J) = 0.
        WK17(J) = .FALSE.
        GOTO 150
C
C       compute WK16 the change in degree of infeasibility
C       corresponding to the change in solution X
C
 100    DO 110 I = 1, LL
           YY1 = WK9(I) + A(I,J)
           IF (YY1 .GT. 0.0)  YY2 = YY2 + YY1
 110    CONTINUE
        GOTO 140
 120    DO 130 I = 1, LL
           YY1 = WK9(I) - A(I,J)
           IF (YY1 .GT. 0.0)  YY2 = YY2 + YY1
 130    CONTINUE
 140    WK16(J) = YY2
        IF (WK16(J) .LE. 0.0)  THEN
           IF (XX2 .GT. XX1)  THEN
              XX1 = XX2
              KK = J
           ENDIF
        ELSE
           IF (YY2 .LT. XWORK)  THEN
              WK17(J) = .TRUE.
              K = J
              INCR = INCR + 1
           ELSE
              WK17(J) = .FALSE.
           ENDIF
        ENDIF
 150 CONTINUE
     IF (KK .NE. 0)  THEN
        X(KK) = X(KK) + WK4(KK)
        RETURN
     ENDIF
C
C    compute the improvement of the objective function
C
     IF (INCR .GT. 0)  THEN
        IF (INCR .GT. 1)  THEN
           TEMP = EPSILN
           DO 160 J = 1, N
              IF (WK17(J))  THEN
                 IF ((XWORK-WK16(J)) .GT. TEMP)  THEN
                    JHIGH = J
                    TEMP = XWORK - WK16(J)
                 ENDIF
              ENDIF
 160       CONTINUE
           K = JHIGH
        ENDIF
        X(K) = X(K) + WK4(K)
        YY1 = WK4(K)
        DO 170 I = 1, LL
 170       WK9(I) = WK9(I) + A(I,K) * YY1
        XWORK = WK16(K)
        GOTO 70
     ENDIF
C
```

```
C     continue with the linear search
C
      DELTA = DELTA + DELPS
      IF (DELTA .LE. 1.0) GOTO 10
C
      RETURN
      END
```

```
      SUBROUTINE PARSE2(N,M,IADIM,A,B,C,X,WK3,WK5,WK10,IWK18)
C
C     This subprogram is used by subroutine INTLP
C
      REAL    A(IADIM,1),B(1),C(1),X(1),WK3(1),WK5(1),WK10(1)
      INTEGER IWK18(1)
      COMMON  /C2/ INIT
C
C     improve the feasible solution by changing some variable by one,
C     this is the initialization part
C
      DO 10 J = 1, N
         IWK18(J) = J
 10      WK3(J) = C(J)
      N1 = N - 1
      DO 30 I = 1, N1
         TEMP = ABS(WK3(I))
         I1 = I + 1
         DO 20 J = I1, N
            IF (ABS(WK3(J)) .GT. TEMP)  THEN
               JJ = IWK18(I)
               IWK18(I) = IWK18(J)
               IWK18(J) = JJ
               TEMP = ABS(WK3(J))
               SWAP = WK3(I)
               WK3(I) = WK3(J)
               WK3(J)= SWAP
            ENDIF
 20      CONTINUE
 30   CONTINUE
      DO 40 J = 1, N
         IF (ABS(WK3(J)) .GT. 0.0)  INIT = J
 40   CONTINUE
C
C     set WK5 to indicate whether the objective coefficient
C     is positive
C
      DO 50 J = 1, INIT
         LL = IWK18(J)
         IF (WK3(J) .NE. 0.0)  THEN
            IF (WK3(J) .LT. 0.0)  THEN
               WK5(LL) = -1.0
            ELSE
               WK5(LL) = 1.0
            ENDIF
         ENDIF
 50   CONTINUE
C
C     compute WK10 the feasibility test slacks
C
      DO 70 I = 1, M
         TEMP = 0.
         DO 60 J = 1, N
 60         TEMP = TEMP + A(I,J) * X(J)
 70      WK10(I) = B(I) - TEMP
C
      RETURN
      END
```

```
      SUBROUTINE PARSE3(N,M,IADIM,A,C,X,BIG,WK10)
C
C     This subprogram is used by subroutine INTLP
C
      REAL    A(IADIM,1),C(1),X(1),WK10(1)
      COMMON  /C1/ J,K
C
C     iteratively change the value of some variable by one to improve
C     the objective value
C
 10   K = 1
      XX1 = 0.
C
C     the variable that gives a large increase in the objective value
C     is chosen to be changed
C
      DO 30 J = 1, N
         IF (C(J) .NE. 0.0)  THEN
            IF ((C(J) .GT. 0.0) .OR. (X(J) .GT. 0.0))  THEN
               TEMP = BIG
               DO 20 I = 1, M
                  IF (C(J)*A(I,J) .GT. 0.0)  THEN
                     XX2 = WK10(I) / ABS(A(I,J))
                     IF (XX2 .LT. 0.0)  THEN
                        IF (XX2 .NE. AINT(XX2)) XX2 = AINT(XX2) - 1.0
                     ELSE
                        IF (XX2 .GT. 0.0)  XX2 = AINT(XX2)
                     ENDIF
                     IF (XX2 .LT. TEMP)  TEMP = XX2
                  ENDIF
 20            CONTINUE
               IF (XX1 .LE. ABS(C(J))*TEMP)  THEN
                  XX1 = ABS(C(J)) * TEMP
                  K = J
               ENDIF
            ENDIF
         ENDIF
 30   CONTINUE
C
C     increase or decrease X(K) by one
C
      IF (XX1 .EQ. 0.0)  RETURN
      IF (C(K) .LE. 0.0)  THEN
         X(K) = X(K) - 1.0
         DO 40 I = 1, M
 40         WK10(I) = WK10(I) + A(I,K)
         GOTO 10
      ENDIF
      X(K) = X(K) + 1.0
      DO 50 I = 1, M
 50      WK10(I) = WK10(I) - A(I,K)
      GOTO 10
C
      END
```

```
      SUBROUTINE PARSE4(N,C,WK1,IWK18)
C
C     This subprogram is used by subroutine INTLP
C
      REAL    C(1),WK1(N,N)
      INTEGER IWK18(1)
      COMMON  /C1/ J,K
      COMMON  /C2/ INIT
C
C     prepare for the interchange of two variables;
C     determine the bounds on the size of changes, the ratios of
C      the objective coefficients are computed and stored in WK1
C
      INIT1 = INIT - 1
      DO 20 J = 1, INIT1
         J1 = J + 1
         J2 = IWK18(J)
         DO 10 K = J1, INIT
            J3 = IWK18(K)
            TEMP = ABS(C(J2) / C(J3))
            IF (TEMP .LE. 1.0)  THEN
               WK1(J,K) = AINT(TEMP - 1.0)
            ELSE
               IF (AINT(TEMP) .EQ. TEMP)  THEN
                  WK1(J,K) = AINT(TEMP - 1.0)
               ELSE
                  WK1(J,K) = AINT(TEMP - 1.0) + 1.0
               ENDIF
            ENDIF
            IF (TEMP .GE. -1.0)  THEN
               WK1(K,J) = AINT(TEMP + 1.0)
            ELSE
               IF (AINT(TEMP) .EQ. TEMP)  THEN
                  WK1(K,J) = AINT(TEMP + 1.0)
               ELSE
                  WK1(K,J) = AINT(TEMP + 1.0) - 1.0
               ENDIF
            ENDIF
 10      CONTINUE
 20   CONTINUE
C
      RETURN
      END
```

```
      SUBROUTINE PARSE5(M,IADIM,A,X,WK5,WK10,WK11,IWK18,MOVEON)
C
C     This subprogram is used by subroutine INTLP
C
      REAL    A(IADIM,1),X(1),WK5(1),WK10(1),WK11(1)
      INTEGER IWK18(1)
      COMMON  /C1/ J,K
C
C     check if the changed value of X(J) is negative
C
      ISUB = IWK18(J)
 10   IF (X(ISUB) .LT. -WK5(ISUB))  THEN
         MOVEON = 0
         RETURN
      ENDIF
C
C     if the change is negative then check whether this change is
C     feasible without changing another variable
C
      ICON = 0
      DO 20 I = 1, M
         WK11(I) = WK10(I) - WK5(ISUB) * A(I,ISUB)
         IF (WK11(I) .LT. 0.0)  ICON = 1
 20   CONTINUE
      IF (ICON .NE. 1)  THEN
         X(ISUB) = X(ISUB) + WK5(ISUB)
         DO 30 I = 1, M
 30         WK10(I) = WK11(I)
         GOTO 10
      ENDIF
      MOVEON = 1
C
      RETURN
      END
```

```
      SUBROUTINE PARSE6(N,M,IADIM,A,C,X,BIG,
     +                  WK1,WK3,WK5,WK10,WK11,IWK18,MORE)
C
C     This subprogram is used by subroutine INTLP
C
      REAL     A(IADIM,1),C(1),X(1),
     +         WK1(N,N),WK3(1),WK5(1),WK10(1),WK11(1)
      INTEGER IWK18(1)
      COMMON  /C1/ J,K
C
C     check for the change of variables X(J) and X(K)
C     and identify a better solution
C
      IF (WK3(K) .GT. 0.0)  THEN
         ISUB = IWK18(K)
         XWK2 = -AMIN1(X(ISUB),WK1(J,K))
      ELSE
         ISUB = IWK18(K)
         XWK2 = -X(ISUB)
      ENDIF
      XWK3 = BIG
      ISUB = IWK18(K)
      DO 10 I = 1, M
         IF (WK11(I) .LT. 0.0)  THEN
            TEMP = WK11(I) / A(I,ISUB)
            IF (TEMP .NE. AINT(TEMP))  TEMP = AINT(TEMP) - 1.0
            IF (TEMP .LT. XWK3)  XWK3 = TEMP
         ENDIF
 10   CONTINUE
C
C     check whether feasibility can be restored
C
      IF (XWK2 .GT. XWK3)  THEN
         MORE = 0
         RETURN
      ENDIF
      ISUB = IWK18(K)
      XWK1 = -BIG
      DO 20 I = 1, M
         IF (A(I,ISUB) .LT. 0.0)  THEN
            TEMP = WK11(I) / A(I,ISUB)
            IF (TEMP .LT. 0.0)  THEN
               TEMP = AINT(TEMP)
            ELSE
               IF (TEMP .GT. 0.0)  THEN
                  IF (TEMP .NE. AINT(TEMP)) TEMP = AINT(TEMP)+1.0
               ENDIF
            ENDIF
            IF (TEMP .GT. XWK1)  XWK1 = TEMP
         ENDIF
 20   CONTINUE
C
C     check if an improved solution can be obtained
C
      IF (XWK1 .GT. XWK2)  XWK2 = XWK1
      IF (XWK2 .GT. XWK3)  THEN
         MORE = 0
         RETURN
      ENDIF
      ISUB = IWK18(K)
      IF (C(ISUB) .LE. 0.0)  THEN
         JSUB = IWK18(J)
         X(JSUB) = X(JSUB) + WK5(JSUB)
```

```
         X(ISUB) = X(ISUB) + XWK2
         DO 30 I = 1, M
 30         WK10(I) = WK11(I) - XWK2 * A(I,ISUB)
         MORE = 1
         RETURN
      ENDIF
C
C     a better solution is obtained
C
      X(ISUB) = X(ISUB) + XWK3
      DO 40 I = 1, M
 40      WK10(I) = WK11(I) - XWK3 * A(I,ISUB)
      ISUB = IWK18(J)
      X(ISUB) = X(ISUB) + WK5(ISUB)
      MORE = 1
C
      RETURN
      END
```

```
      SUBROUTINE PARSE7(N,M,IADIM,A,C,X,BIG,
     +                  WK1,WK3,WK5,WK10,WK11,IWK18,MORE)
C
C     This subroutine is used by subroutine INTLP
C
      REAL    A(IADIM,1),C(1),X(1),
     +        WK1(N,N),WK3(1),WK5(1),WK10(1),WK11(1)
      INTEGER IWK18(1)
      COMMON  /C1/ J,K
C
C     try to increase X(K) to get a better solution
C
 10   IF (WK3(K) .LT. 0.0)  THEN
         XWK1 = WK1(J,K)
      ELSE
         XWK1 = BIG
      ENDIF
      ISUB = IWK18(K)
      TEMP = -BIG
      DO 20 I = 1, M
         IF (WK11(I) .LT. 0.0)  THEN
            XWORK = WK11(I) / A(I,ISUB)
            IF (AINT(XWORK) .NE. XWORK)  XWORK = AINT(XWORK) + 1.0
            IF (TEMP .LT. XWORK)  TEMP = XWORK
         ENDIF
 20   CONTINUE
C
C     check whether feasibility can be restored
C
      XWK2 = TEMP
      IF (XWK2 .GT. XWK1)  THEN
         MORE = 0
         RETURN
      ENDIF
      ISUB = IWK18(K)
      TEMP = BIG
      DO 30 I = 1, M
         IF (A(I,ISUB) .GT. 0.0)  THEN
            XWORK = WK11(I) / A(I,ISUB)
            IF (XWORK .GT. 0.0)  THEN
               XWORK = AINT(XWORK)
            ELSE
               IF (XWORK .LT. 0.0)  THEN
                  IF (XWORK .NE. AINT(XWORK))
     +               XWORK = AINT(XWORK) - 1.0
               ENDIF
            ENDIF
            IF (TEMP .GT. XWORK)  TEMP = XWORK
         ENDIF
 30   CONTINUE
C
C     check if an improved solution can be obtained
C
      IF (TEMP .LT. XWK1)  XWK1 = TEMP
      IF (XWK2 .GT. XWK1)  THEN
         MORE = 0
         RETURN
      ENDIF
      ISUB = IWK18(K)
      IF (C(ISUB) .LE. 0.0)  THEN
         JSUB = IWK18(J)
         X(JSUB) = X(JSUB) + WK5(JSUB)
         X(ISUB) = X(ISUB) + XWK2
```

```
         DO 40 I = 1, M
 40         WK10(I) = WK11(I) - XWK2 * A(I,ISUB)
         MORE = 1
         RETURN
      ENDIF
C
C     a better solution is found
C
      X(ISUB) = X(ISUB) + XWK1
      DO 50 I = 1, M
 50      WK10(I) = WK11(I) - XWK1 * A(I,ISUB)
      ISUB = IWK18(J)
      X(ISUB) = X(ISUB) + WK5(ISUB)
      MORE = 1
C
      RETURN
      END
```

```
      SUBROUTINE PARSE8(N,M,IADIM,A,X,WK1,WK5,WK10,WK11,IWK18)
C
C     This subprogram is used by subroutine INTLP
C
      REAL    A(IADIM,1),X(1),
     +        WK1(N,N),WK5(1),WK10(1),WK11(1)
      INTEGER IWK18(1)
      COMMON  /C1/ J,K
      COMMON  /C2/ INIT
C
C     consider changing X(J) and a small integer change of X(K)
C
 10   ISUB = IWK18(J)
      IF (X(ISUB) .LT. WK5(ISUB))  RETURN
      DO 20 I = 1, M
 20      WK11(I) = WK10(I) + WK5(ISUB) * A(I,ISUB)
 30   IF (K .GT. INIT)  RETURN
C
C     check whether the simultaneous change of X(J) and X(K)
C        is feasible
C
      ISUB = IWK18(K)
      IF ((X(ISUB)+WK5(ISUB)*WK1(K,J)) .LT. 0.0)  THEN
         K = K + 1
         GOTO 30
      ENDIF
      ISUB = IWK18(K)
      DO 40 I = 1, M
         IF ((WK11(I)-WK5(ISUB)*WK1(K,J)*A(I,ISUB)) .LT. 0.0) THEN
            K = K + 1
            GOTO 30
         ENDIF
 40   CONTINUE
C
C     make the simultaneous change of X(J) and X(K)
C
      ISUB = IWK18(J)
      X(ISUB) = X(ISUB) - WK5(ISUB)
      ISUB = IWK18(K)
      X(ISUB) = X(ISUB) + WK5(ISUB) * WK1(K,J)
      DO 50 I = 1, M
 50      WK10(I) = WK11(I) - WK5(ISUB) * WK1(K,J) * A(I,ISUB)
      GOTO 10
C
      END
```

Chapter 2

ZERO-ONE LINEAR PROGRAMMING

A. Problem Description

Consider the zero-one linear programming problem

$$\text{maximize} \qquad Z = \sum_{j=1}^{n} c_j x_j$$

$$\text{subject to} \qquad \sum_{j=1}^{n} a_{ij} x_j \le b_i \qquad (i=1,2,\ldots,m)$$

$$x_j = 0,\ 1 \qquad (j=1,2,\ldots,n)$$

such that all the data a_{ij}, b_i, c_j are nonnegative.

This is also known as the *multi-dimensional knapsack type zero-one programming problem*. In general, there are n given items, and m restricted resources. The number c_j represents the value of item j, b_i represents the upper limit on resource i and a_{ij} represents the amount of resource i consumed by item j. The problem is to choose a set of valuable items while satisfying the limitations of restricted resources. The decision $x_i = 1$ means that the item i is accepted and $x_i = 0$ means that the item i is rejected.

The heuristic procedure to be described provides a good approximate solution. It is particularly effective for solving large size problems.

Let J = set of all n items, i.e., $J = \{1,2,\ldots,n\}$,

S = set of accepted items,

T = set of items not in S, i.e., $T = J - S$,

R = m-vector of the cumulative total resource vector required by the set of accepted items.

B. Algorithm

Step 1. Compute the ratios

$$d_{ij} = a_{ij} / b_i$$

for $i=1,2,\dots,m$ and $j=1,2,\dots,n$.

Let D_j be the resource requirement vector for item j,

i.e., $D_j = (d_{1j}, d_{2j}, \dots, d_{mj})$; and

B be the normalized limit vector of resources,

i.e., B is an m-vector of all ones.

Initialize

$$S = \emptyset, \quad T = J, \quad R = \text{zero vector},$$
$$x_j = 0 \quad \text{for } j=1,2,\dots,n, \quad \text{and} \quad Z = 0.$$

Step 2. Let U be the set of all eligible items, i.e.,

$$U = \{i : i \in T \text{ and } D_i \le B - R\} .$$

If U is empty then stop.

Step 3. Compute the effective gradients g_j for the elements in U as follows.
If R is a zero vector then set

$$g_j = m^{1/2} c_j / \sum_{i=1}^{m} d_{ij} \qquad \text{for} \quad j \in U,$$

otherwise compute

$$f_i = \sum_{j \in S} d_{ij} ,$$

$$g_j = c_j \left(\sum_{i=1}^{m} f_i^2 \right)^{1/2} / \left(\sum_{i=1}^{m} d_{ij} f_i \right) \qquad \text{for} \quad j \in U;$$

in the case when $\sum_{i=1}^{m} d_{ij} f_i = 0$ then set $g_j = \infty$.

Step 4. Among the effective gradients, let g_k be the largest.
Set

$$S = S + \{k\}, \quad T = T - \{k\}, \quad R = R + D_k,$$
$$Z = Z + c_k, \quad x_k = 1.$$

Go to Step 2.

C. Subroutine MULKNP Parameters

Input :

M - number of constraints.

N - number of variables.

A - real matrix of dimension M by N containing the coefficients of the M constraints; on output, the matrix A is modified.

B - real vector of length M containing the right hand sides of the constraints.

C - real vector of length N containing the coefficients of the objective function.

IADIM - row dimension of matrix A exactly as specified in the dimension statement of the calling program.

Output :

Z - value of the objective function.

NUMSOL - number of nonzero variables in the solution.

ISOL - integer vector of length N; the nonzero variables of the solution are stored in

ISOL(i), i=1,2,...,NUMSOL.

Working Storages :

WK1 - real vector of length M; total quantity of restricted resource i required by the set of accepted variables, i=1,2,...,M.

WK2 - real vector of length M; penalty vector.

IWK3 - integer vector of length N; set of candidate variables.

D. Test Example

$$\text{maximize} \quad 31x_1 + 26x_2 + 27x_3 + 29x_4 + 32x_5 + 30x_6 + 28x_7$$

$$\text{subject to} \quad 4x_1 + 5x_2 + 3x_3 + 3x_4 + 7x_5 + 8x_6 + 8x_7 \le 19$$

$$3x_1 + 7x_2 + 4x_3 + 9x_4 + 8x_5 + 5x_6 + 6x_7 \le 14$$

$$3x_1 + x_2 + 2x_3 + 5x_4 + 4x_5 + 4x_6 + 6x_7 \le 17$$

$$x_j = 0 \text{ or } 1, \quad j = 1, 2, \ldots, 7.$$

Main Program

```
      INTEGER ISOL(7),IWK3(7)
      REAL    A(3,7),B(3),C(7),WK1(3),WK2(3)
C
      READ(*,10) M,N
 10   FORMAT(2I5)
      DO 20 I = 1 , M
 20      READ(*,30) (A(I,J),J=1,N)
 30      FORMAT(7F8.0)
      READ(*,30) (B(I),I=1,M)
      READ(*,30) (C(I),I=1,N)
      IADIM = 3
C
      CALL MULKNP(M,N,A,B,C,IADIM,Z,NUMSOL,ISOL,WK1,WK2,IWK3)
C
      WRITE(*,40) Z,(ISOL(J),J=1,NUMSOL)
 40   FORMAT(/'  THE OBJECTIVE FUNCTION VALUE  :',F8.1,
     +      //'     THE NONZERO VARIABLES ARE  :',7I3)
      STOP
      END
```

Input Data

```
    3    7
      4.      5.      3.      3.      7.      8.      8.
      3.      7.      4.      9.      8.      5.      6.
      3.      1.      2.      5.      4.      4.      6.
     19.     14.     17.
     31.     26.     27.     29.     32.     30.     28.
```

Output Results

```
  THE OBJECTIVE FUNCTION VALUE  :    88.0

     THE NONZERO VARIABLES ARE  :  1  3  6
```

```
      SUBROUTINE MULKNP (M,N,A,B,C,IADIM,Z,NUMSOL,ISOL,WK1,WK2,IWK3)
C
C     Multi-dimensional zero-one knapsack heuristic
C
      INTEGER ISOL(N),IWK3(N)
      REAL    A(IADIM,1),B(M),C(N),Z,WK1(M),WK2(M)
      LOGICAL CHECK
C
C     compute the machine epsilon
C
      EPS = 1.0
 10   EPS = EPS / 2.0
         TOL   = 1.0 + EPS
         IF (TOL .GT. 1.0)  GO TO 10
      EPS = SQRT(EPS)
C
C     compute the machine infinity
C
      BIG = 1.0E6
 20   BIG = BIG * BIG
         TOL = 1.0 + BIG
         IF (TOL .GT. BIG)  GO TO 20
      BIG = BIG * BIG
      SMALL = 1.0 / BIG
C
C     initialize
C
      DO 40 I = 1, M
         RECIPB = 1.0 / B(I)
         DO 30 J = 1, N
 30         A(I,J) = A(I,J) * RECIPB
         WK1(I) = 0.0
 40   CONTINUE
      Z = 0.0
      NUMSOL = 0
      DO 50 J = 1, N
 50      IWK3(J) = J
C
      ROOTM  = SQRT(FLOAT(M))
      NUMCAN = N
 60   NCAN   = NUMCAN
      NUMCAN = 0
      GRDMAX = -BIG
C
C     when the resource requirement vector is zero
C
      DO 90 J = 1, NCAN
C
C        select variables
C
         JJ = IWK3(J)
         DO 70 I = 1, M
            IF ((WK1(I) + A(I,JJ) - 1.0) .GT. EPS)  GO TO 90
 70      CONTINUE
         NUMCAN = NUMCAN + 1
         IWK3(NUMCAN) = JJ
C
C        compute the effective gradients
C
         SUM = 0.0
         DO 80 I = 1, M
            SUM = SUM + A(I,JJ)
 80      CONTINUE
```

```
         IF (SUM .LE. SMALL)  THEN
            GRAD = BIG
         ELSE
            GRAD = C(JJ) * ROOTM / SUM
         ENDIF
C
C        find the variable whose effective gradient is the largest
C
         IF (GRAD .GT. GRDMAX)  THEN
            GRDMAX = GRAD
            JGDMAX = JJ
            JGM = NUMCAN
         ENDIF
 90   CONTINUE
C
C     accept the variable whose effective gradient is the largest
C
      IF (NUMCAN .LE. 0)  RETURN
      IF (NUMCAN .EQ. 1)  THEN
         Z = Z + C(JGDMAX)
         DO 100 I = 1, M
            WK1(I) = WK1(I) + A(I,JGDMAX)
 100     CONTINUE
         NUMSOL = NUMSOL + 1
         ISOL(NUMSOL) = JGDMAX
         RETURN
      ENDIF
C
      Z = Z + C(JGDMAX)
      NUMSOL = NUMSOL + 1
      ISOL(NUMSOL) = JGDMAX
      IWK3(JGM) = IWK3(NUMCAN)
      NUMCAN = NUMCAN - 1
      CHECK = .TRUE.
      DO 110 I = 1, M
         WK1(I) = WK1(I) + A(I,JGDMAX)
         IF (WK1(I) .GT. EPS)  CHECK = .FALSE.
 110  CONTINUE
      IF (CHECK) GO TO 60
C
 120  CMAX = WK1(1)
      DO 130 I = 2, M
         IF (WK1(I) .GT. CMAX)  CMAX = WK1(I)
 130  CONTINUE
      ORIMOV = CMAX * CMAX
      SUMSQ = 0.0
      DO 140 I = 1, M
         WK2(I) = WK1(I) - ORIMOV
         IF (WK2(I) .LE. EPS)  WK2(I) = 0.0
         SUMSQ = SUMSQ + WK2(I) * WK2(I)
 140  CONTINUE
      SUMSQ = SQRT(SUMSQ)
      NCAN = NUMCAN
      NUMCAN = 0
      GRDMAX = -BIG
C
C     when the resource requirement vector is non-zero
C
      DO 170 J = 1, NCAN
C
C        select variables
C
         JJ = IWK3(J)
```

```
        DO 150 I = 1, M
           IF (WK1(I) + A(I,JJ) - 1.0 .GT. EPS) GO TO 170
 150    CONTINUE
        NUMCAN = NUMCAN + 1
        IWK3(NUMCAN) = JJ
C
C       compute effective gradients
C
        SUM = 0.0
        DO 160 I = 1, M
           SUM = SUM + A(I,JJ) * WK2(I)
 160    CONTINUE
        IF (SUM .LE. SMALL)  THEN
           GRAD = BIG
        ELSE
           GRAD = C(JJ) * SUMSQ / SUM
        ENDIF
C
C       find the variable whose effective gradient is the largest
C
        IF (GRAD .GT. GRDMAX)  THEN
           GRDMAX = GRAD
           JGDMAX = JJ
           JGM = NUMCAN
        ENDIF
 170  CONTINUE
C
C     accept the variable whose effective gradient is the largest
C
      IF (NUMCAN .LE. 0)  RETURN
      IF (NUMCAN .EQ. 1)  THEN
        Z = Z + C(JGDMAX)
        DO 180 I = 1, M
           WK1(I) = WK1(I) + A(I,JGDMAX)
 180    CONTINUE
        NUMSOL = NUMSOL + 1
        ISOL(NUMSOL) = JGDMAX
        RETURN
      ENDIF
      Z = Z + C(JGDMAX)
      NUMSOL = NUMSOL + 1
      ISOL(NUMSOL) = JGDMAX
      IWK3(JGM) = IWK3(NUMCAN)
      NUMCAN = NUMCAN - 1
      DO 190 I = 1, M
        WK1(I) = WK1(I) + A(I,JGDMAX)
 190  CONTINUE
      GO TO 120
C
      END
```

Chapter 3

ZERO-ONE KNAPSACK PROBLEM

A. Problem Description

The *zero-one knapsack problem* has the form

$$\text{maximize} \quad \sum_{j=1}^{n} c_j x_j$$

$$\text{subject to} \quad \sum_{j=1}^{n} a_j x_j \le b$$

$$x_j = 0 \text{ or } 1 \qquad (j=1,2,\ldots,n)$$

such that a_j, b and c_j are nonnegative numbers.

Intuitively the ratio

$$c_j \;/\; a_j$$

indicates the desirability of setting $x_j = 1$ in an optimal solution. Naturally, a simple heuristic algorithm is to reorder the variables so that

$$c_1/a_1 \ge c_2/a_2 \ge \ldots \ge c_n/a_n \;.$$

Then an approximate solution can be obtained by setting

$$\bar{x}_i = \begin{cases} 1 & \text{if } a_i + \sum_{j=1}^{i-1} a_j \bar{x}_j \le b \\ 0 & \text{otherwise.} \end{cases}$$

This is the so-called *greedy* heuristic approach.

Let Z_{opt} be the optimal solution of the zero-one knapsack problem, and Z_g be the solution computed by the greedy heuristic procedure. The relation

$$Z_g \geq Z_{opt} - \max c_j$$

shows how close a greedy solution comes to an optimal one.

In the next section, a more sophisticated heuristic algorithm will be described. Within polynomial time, the approximate algorithm finds a solution arbitrarily close to the optimum. More specifically, the algorithm receives an input positive number EPS, and delivers a solution Z_h with

$$Z_h \geq (1 - EPS)\, Z_{opt}$$

requiring only

$$O(n \log n) + O(n / EPS^2)$$

arithmetical operations.

B. Algorithm

Step 1. Reorder the variables so that

$$c_1/a_1 \geq c_2/a_2 \geq \ldots \geq c_n/a_n .$$

Let i be the largest subscript such that

$$a_1 + a_2 + \ldots + a_i \leq b .$$

Define

$$r = c_1 + c_2 + \ldots + c_{i+1} ,$$

$$p = r(EPS / 3)^2 ,$$

$$q = r(EPS / 3).$$

Step 2. Split all variables into two groups S and T :

$$j \in S \quad \text{if} \quad c_j \geq q \quad \text{and}$$

$$j \in T \quad \text{if} \quad c_j < q.$$

Step 3. Solve the sequence of problems

$$\text{minimize} \quad \sum_{j \in S} a_j x_j$$

$$\text{subject to} \quad \sum_{j \in S} \lfloor c_j / p \rfloor \, x_j = d$$

$$x_j = 0, 1 \qquad (j \in S)$$

with d varying over $0, 1, \ldots, \lfloor r/p \rfloor$.

Step 4. For each value of d such that the problem in Step 3 has an optimal solution

$$\bar{x}_j \qquad (j \in S)$$

satisfying

$$\Sigma \, a_j \bar{x}_j \le b \, ,$$

consider the knapsack problem

$$\text{maximize} \quad \sum_{j \in T} c_j x_j$$

$$\text{subject to} \quad \sum_{j \in T} a_j x_j \le b - \sum_{j \in S} a_j \bar{x}_j$$

$$x_j = 0, 1 \qquad (j \in T).$$

The greedy solution

$$\bar{x}_j \qquad (j \in T)$$

of this problem combining with

$$\bar{x}_j \qquad (j \in S)$$

forms a candidate solution of the original zero-one knapsack problem. There are at most

$$1 + \lfloor r/p \rfloor$$

candidates. The best of them is returned as the final solution.

Remarks

Note that in Step 3, it is necessary to solve efficiently a sequence of problems of the form

$$\text{minimize} \quad \sum_{j=1}^{v} a_j x_j$$

$$\text{subject to} \quad \sum_{j=1}^{v} g_j x_j = d$$

$$x_j = 0,\ 1 \qquad (j=1,2,\dots,v)$$

with d varying over $0,1,\dots,m$, where a_j and g_j are nonnegative.

This can be achieved by solving all problems

$$\text{PP :} \quad \text{minimize} \quad \sum_{j=1}^{k} a_j x_j$$

$$\text{subject to} \quad \sum_{j=1}^{k} g_j x_j = d$$

$$x_j = 0,\ 1 \qquad (j=1,2,\dots,k)$$

with $1 \le k \le v$ and $0 \le d \le m$. Let $z(k,d)$ be the optimal value of the objective function in problem PP. The solutions to the problems in PP can be found recursively :

$$z(1,d) = \begin{cases} 0 & \text{if } d = 0 \\ a_1 & \text{if } d = g_1 \\ \infty & \text{otherwise} \end{cases},$$

$$z(k,0) = 0 \quad \text{for all } k,$$

$$z(k,d) = \min \begin{cases} z(k-1,d) \\ z(k-1,d-g_k) + a_k \end{cases}.$$

C. Subroutine KNAPP Parameters

Input :

N - number of variables.

A - real vector of length N containing the coefficients of the constraint.

B - right hand side of the constraint.

C - real vector of length N containing the coefficients of the objective function.

EPS - a positive real number prescribing the required degree of accuracy in the solution.

M - smallest integer greater than $(3 / EPS)^2$.

Output :

OBJVAL - value of the objective function.

NUMSOL - number of nonzero variables in the solution.

ISOL - integer vector of length N; the nonzero variables are stored in ISOL(i), i=1,2,...,NUMSOL.

Working Storages :

WORK1 - real matrix of dimension 2 by M; stores the objective value of subproblems.

WORK2 - real matrix of dimension 2 by M; stores the values of the original objective function for the corresponding subproblems.

WORK3 - real vector of length N; vector of constraints for variables in group one.

WORK4 - real vector of length N; objective coefficients for variables in group two.

WORK5 - real vector of length N; vector of constraints for variables in group two.

IWK1 - integer vector of length N; pointer to the original variable index.

IWK2 - integer vector of length N; pointer to the original variable index for group one variables.

IWK3 - integer vector of length N;
pointer to the original variable index for group two variables.

IWK4 - integer vector of length N;
objective coefficients for group one variables.

IWK5 - boolean vector of length M;
IWK5(i) indicates whether subproblem i has been investigated.

IWK6 - integer vector of length M;
indices for subproblems.

IWK7 - integer matrix of dimension N by M;
stores solutions of subproblems.

Note that subroutine KNAPP calls on a sorting procedure SORTD which uses the heapsort method to sort a given array in nonincreasing order. The parameters of SORTD are described next.

Subroutine SORTD Parameters

Input :

N - number of elements.

A - real vector of length N containing the elements to be sorted.

Output :

A - array containing the elements in nonincreasing order.

IPOINT - integer vector of length N pointing to the original locations of the sorted elements.

Remarks :

Note that the array A is used as both input and output. If the original locations of the input elements are not needed after the sorting, then the array IPOINT can be erased everywhere from the subroutine.

D. Test Example

$$\text{maximize} \quad 442x_1 + 525x_2 + 511x_3 + 593x_4 + 546x_5 + 564x_6 + 617x_7$$

$$\text{subject to} \quad 41x_1 + 50x_2 + 49x_3 + 59x_4 + 55x_5 + 57x_6 + 68x_7 \le 170$$

$$x_j = 0 \text{ or } 1 \quad (j=1,2,\ldots,7).$$

The problem is to be solved with the degree of accuracy

$$\text{EPS} = 0.8 \; .$$

Main Program

```
      INTEGER ISOL(7),IWK1(7),IWK2(7),IWK3(7),IWK4(7),
     +        IWK6(15),IWK7(7,15)
      REAL    A(7),C(7),WORK1(2,15),WORK2(2,15),
     +        WORK3(7),WORK4(7),WORK5(7)
      LOGICAL IWK5(15)
C
      READ(*,10) N
 10   FORMAT(I4)
      READ(*,20) (A(I),I=1,N)
      READ(*,20) B
      READ(*,20) (C(I),I=1,N)
 20   FORMAT(7F5.0)
      EPS = 0.8
      M = 15
      CALL KNAPP (N,A,B,C,EPS,M,OBJVAL,NUMSOL,ISOL,
     +            WORK1,WORK2,WORK3,WORK4,WORK5,
     +            IWK1,IWK2,IWK3,IWK4,IWK5,IWK6,IWK7)
C
      WRITE(*,30) OBJVAL,(ISOL(I),I=1,NUMSOL)
 30   FORMAT(/' OBJECTIVE FUNCTION VALUE :',F10.1/
     +       /'          NONZERO VARIABLES :',7I4)
      STOP
      END
```

Input Data

```
   7
  41.  50.  49.  59.  55.  57.  68.
 170.
 442. 525. 511. 593. 546. 564. 617.
```

Output Results

```
 OBJECTIVE FUNCTION VALUE :     1652.0

          NONZERO VARIABLES :   7   4   1
```

```
      SUBROUTINE KNAPP (N,A,B,C,EPS,M,OBJVAL,NUMSOL,ISOL,
     +                  WORK1,WORK2,WORK3,WORK4,WORK5,
     +                  IWK1,IWK2,IWK3,IWK4,IWK5,IWK6,IWK7)
C
C     zero-one knapsack heuristic
C
      INTEGER ISOL(N),IWK1(N),IWK2(N),IWK3(N),IWK4(N),
     +        IWK6(M),IWK7(N,M)
      REAL    A(N),C(N),WORK1(2,M),WORK2(2,M),
     +        WORK3(N),WORK4(N),WORK5(N)
      LOGICAL IWK5(M),SWITCH
C
C     reorder the variables
C
      BIG = 1.0
      DO 10 I = 1, N
         WORK3(I) = C(I) / A(I)
 10      BIG = BIG + C(I)
C
      CALL SORTD(N,WORK3,IWK1)
C
C     calculate the initial parameters
C
      NUMSOL = 0
      OBJVAL = 0.
      RHS = B
      J = 1
 20   INDEX = IWK1(J)
      IF (RHS .GE. A(INDEX))  THEN
         RHS = RHS - A(INDEX)
         J = J + 1
         IF (J .LE. N)  GOTO 20
      ENDIF
      IF (J .GT. N)  THEN
         NUMSOL = N
         DO 30 I = 1, N
            OBJVAL = OBJVAL + C(J)
 30         ISOL(I) = I
         RETURN
      ENDIF
      EST = 0.
      DO 40 I = 1, J
         INDEX = IWK1(I)
 40      EST = EST + C(INDEX)
      XTEMP = EPS / 3.0
      PARM2 = XTEMP * EST
      PARM1 = XTEMP * PARM2
C
C     split the variables into two groups
C
      IGP1 = 0
      IGP2 = 0
      DO 50 I = 1, N
         INDEX = IWK1(I)
         IF (C(INDEX) .GE. PARM2)  THEN
            IGP1= IGP1 + 1
            IWK4(IGP1) = C(INDEX) / PARM1
            WORK3(IGP1) = A(INDEX)
            IWK2(IGP1) = INDEX
         ELSE
            IGP2= IGP2 + 1
            WORK5(IGP2) = A(INDEX)
            WORK4(IGP2) = C(INDEX)
```

```
            IWK3(IGP2) = INDEX
         ENDIF
 50   CONTINUE
C
      IF ((IGP1 .EQ. 0) .OR. (M .LE. 1))  THEN
         RHS = B
         J = 1
 60      INDEX = IWK1(J)
         IF (RHS .GE. A(INDEX))  THEN
            NUMSOL = NUMSOL + 1
            ISOL(NUMSOL) = INDEX
            OBJVAL = OBJVAL + C(INDEX)
            RHS = RHS - A(INDEX)
         ENDIF
         J = J + 1
         IF (J .LE. N)  GOTO 60
         RETURN
      ENDIF
C
C     solve the sequence of problems in group one
C
      WORK1(1,1) = 0.
      WORK1(2,1) = 0.
      WORK2(1,1) = 0.
      WORK2(2,1) = 0.
      DO 70 I = 2, M
         WORK1(1,I) = BIG
 70      WORK2(1,I) = 0.
      I = IWK4(1) + 1
      WORK1(1,I) = WORK3(1)
      INDEX = IWK2(1)
      WORK2(1,I) = C(INDEX)
      SWITCH = .TRUE.
      ICOL2 = 1
      K = 2
 80   IF (K .LE. IGP1)  THEN
         IF (SWITCH)  THEN
            ICOL1 = 1
            ICOL2 = 2
         ELSE
            ICOL1 = 2
            ICOL2 = 1
         ENDIF
         SWITCH = .NOT. SWITCH
         DO 90 I = 2, M
            IROW = I - 1 - IWK4(K)
            IF (IROW .LT. 0)  THEN
               XTEMP = BIG
            ELSE
               IROW = IROW + 1
               XTEMP = WORK1(ICOL1,IROW)
               IF (XTEMP .LT. BIG)  XTEMP = XTEMP + WORK3(K)
            ENDIF
            YTEMP = WORK1(ICOL1,I)
            IF (YTEMP .LE. XTEMP)  THEN
               WORK1(ICOL2,I) = YTEMP
               WORK2(ICOL2,I) = WORK2(ICOL1,I)
            ELSE
               WORK1(ICOL2,I) = XTEMP
               INDEX = IWK2(K)
               WORK2(ICOL2,I) = WORK2(ICOL1,IROW) + C(INDEX)
            ENDIF
 90      CONTINUE
```

```
            K = K + 1
            GOTO 80
         ENDIF
C
C        find the maximum objective value
C
         DO 110 I = 1, M
            VALUE = WORK1(ICOL2,I)
            IF (VALUE .LE. B)  THEN
               GVALUE = 0.
               IF (IGP2 .GT. 0)  THEN
                  RHS = B - VALUE
                  IF (RHS .LT. 0)  THEN
                     WORK2(ICOL2,I) = 0.
                  ELSE
                     J = 1
  100                IF (RHS .GE. WORK5(J))  THEN
                        GVALUE = GVALUE + WORK4(J)
                        RHS = RHS - WORK5(J)
                     ENDIF
                     J = J + 1
                     IF (J .LE. IGP2)  GOTO 100
                  ENDIF
               ENDIF
               GVALUE = GVALUE + WORK2(ICOL2,I)
               IF (GVALUE .GT. OBJVAL)  THEN
                  OBJVAL = GVALUE
                  ISUB = I
               ENDIF
            ENDIF
  110    CONTINUE
C
C        obtain the best solution
C
         IF (ISUB .EQ. 1)  THEN
            IF (IGP2 .GT. 0)  THEN
               RHS = B
               J = 1
  120          INDEX = IWK3(J)
                  IF (RHS .GE. WORK5(J))  THEN
                     NUMSOL = NUMSOL + 1
                     ISOL(NUMSOL) = INDEX
                     RHS = RHS - WORK5(J)
                  ENDIF
                  J = J + 1
               IF (J .LE. IGP2)  GOTO 120
            ENDIF
            RETURN
         ENDIF
C
         DO 130 I = 1, M
            IWK5(I) = .FALSE.
  130       IWK6(I) = 0
         WORK1(1,1) = 0.
         WORK1(2,1) = 0.
         WORK2(1,1) = 0.
         DO 140 I = 2, ISUB
  140       WORK1(1,I) = BIG
         I = IWK4(1) + 1
         WORK1(1,I) = WORK3(1)
         IWK6(I) = 1
         IWK7(1,I) = 1
C
```

```
      SWITCH = .TRUE.
      ICOL2 = 1
      K = 2
 150  IF (K .LE. IGP1)  THEN
         IF (SWITCH)  THEN
            ICOL1 = 1
            ICOL2 = 2
         ELSE
            ICOL1 = 2
            ICOL2 = 1
         ENDIF
         SWITCH = .NOT. SWITCH
         DO 160 I = 2, ISUB
            IROW = I - 1 - IWK4(K)
            IF (IROW .LT. 0)  THEN
               XTEMP = BIG
            ELSE
               IROW = IROW + 1
               XTEMP = WORK1(ICOL1,IROW)
               IF (XTEMP .LT. BIG)  THEN
                  XTEMP = XTEMP + WORK3(K)
               ENDIF
            ENDIF
            YTEMP = WORK1(ICOL1,I)
            IF (YTEMP .LE. XTEMP)  THEN
               WORK1(ICOL2,I) = YTEMP
            ELSE
               WORK1(ICOL2,I) = XTEMP
            ENDIF
            IF (WORK1(ICOL1,I) .NE. WORK1(ICOL2,I))  IWK5(I) = .TRUE.
 160     CONTINUE
         DO 180 II = 2, ISUB
            I = ISUB - II + 2
            IF (IWK5(I))  THEN
               IWK5(I) = .FALSE.
               IROW = I - IWK4(K)
               J = IWK6(IROW)
 170           IF (J .GT. 0)  THEN
                  IWK7(J,I) = IWK7(J,IROW)
                  J = J - 1
                  GOTO 170
               ENDIF
               INDEX = IWK6(IROW) + 1
               IWK6(I) = INDEX
               IWK7(INDEX,I) = K
            ENDIF
 180     CONTINUE
         K = K + 1
         GOTO 150
      ENDIF
C
      J = IWK6(ISUB)
 190  IF (J .GT. 0)  THEN
         NUMSOL = NUMSOL + 1
         INDEX = IWK7(J,ISUB)
         ISOL(NUMSOL) = IWK2(INDEX)
         J = J - 1
         GOTO 190
      ENDIF
C
      IF (IGP2 .GT. 0)  THEN
         RHS = B - WORK1(ICOL2,ISUB)
         J = 1
```

```
200     IF (RHS .GE. WORK5(J))  THEN
           NUMSOL = NUMSOL + 1
           ISOL(NUMSOL) = IWK3(J)
           RHS = RHS - WORK5(J)
        ENDIF
        J = J + 1
        IF (J .LE. IGP2)  GOTO 200
      ENDIF
C
      RETURN
      END
```

```
      SUBROUTINE SORTD (N,A,IPOINT)
C
C     Heapsort :  nonincreasing order sorting
C
      INTEGER  IPOINT(N)
      REAL     A(N)
C
      DO 10 I = 1, N
 10      IPOINT(I) = I
      J1 = N
      J2 = N / 2
      J3 = J2
      ATEMP = A(J2)
      JPONT = IPOINT(J2)
 20   J4 = J2 + J2
      IF (J4 .LE. J1)  THEN
         IF (J4 .LT. J1)  THEN
            IF (A(J4+1) .LT. A(J4))  J4 = J4 + 1
         ENDIF
         IF (ATEMP .GE. A(J4))  THEN
            A(J2) = A(J4)
            IPOINT(J2) = IPOINT(J4)
            J2 = J4
            GOTO 20
         ENDIF
      ENDIF
      A(J2) = ATEMP
      IPOINT(J2) = JPONT
      IF (J3 .GT. 1)  THEN
         J3 = J3 - 1
         ATEMP = A(J3)
         JPONT = IPOINT(J3)
         J2 = J3
         GOTO 20
      ENDIF
      IF (J1 .GE. 2)  THEN
         ATEMP = A(J1)
         JPONT = IPOINT(J1)
         A(J1) = A(1)
         IPOINT(J1) = IPOINT(1)
         J1 = J1 - 1
         J2 = J3
         GOTO 20
      ENDIF
C
      RETURN
      END
```

Chapter 4

TRAVELING SALESMAN PROBLEM

A. Problem Description

Let G be a complete graph with an associated distance matrix (d_{ij}) on its edges. The *traveling salesman problem* is to start from a node in G, visit every other node exactly once and return back to the starting node in such a way that the total traveled distance is minimum. In graph terminology, the traveling salesman problem is to find the least cost Hamiltonian circuit in a given undirected graph.

In general, it is very hard to develop efficient algorithms that yield good approximate solutions to the problem. However, in the particular case when the distance matrix is symmetric and the triangle inequality is satisfied, i.e.,

$$d_{ij} + d_{jk} \geq d_{ik} \qquad \text{for all} \quad 1 \leq i,j,k \leq n,$$

where n is the number of nodes in the graph, then solutions close to the optimum can be found in a relatively short computer time. In fact, the algorithm to be described next guarantees to find a circuit of length no worse than 3/2 of the optimum length in polynomial time.

B. Algorithm

Step 1. Construct a minimum spanning tree T with distance matrix (d_{ij}) in G.

Step 2. Let V be the set of nodes with odd degrees in the minimum spanning tree (there must be an even number of such nodes). Determine a minimum weight perfect matching P of the nodes in V.
Let H be the multigraph of T + P.

Step 3. Construct an Euler circuit in H.
Let the nodes in the Euler circuit be given by the expression

$$(v_1, v_2, \ldots, v_m, v_1).$$

Step 4. Convert this Euler circuit into a Hamiltonian circuit as follows.

a. Scan the expression

$$(v_1, v_2, \ldots, v_m, v_1)$$

from left to right searching for the first node which appear for a second time. Call this node v_f.

b. If $v_f = v_1$ then stop.

c. Delete the nodes

$$v_f, v_{f+1}, \ldots, v_g,$$

where all nodes

$$v_f, v_{f+1}, \ldots, v_g$$

appear earlier in the expression and v_{g+1} does not.
This corresponds to replacing the path

$$v_{f-1}, v_f, \ldots, v_g, v_{g+1}$$

in the Euler circuit by a new branch v_{f-1}, v_{g+1}.
By the triangle inequality rule, the length of the path removed is greater than the length of the new branch.
Return to Step 4a.

Remarks

Let L be the length of the optimum solution. The total length of the branches in H constructed in Step 2 is at most 1/2 of L. Thus the Euler circuit constructed in Step 3 is no longer than 3/2 of L. The Hamiltonian circuit constructed in Step 4 is no longer than the Euler circuit. Therefore, the algorithm always delivers a solution with length at most 3/2 of the optimum length.

Subroutine TSP calls on three auxiliary procedures :

a. Subroutine MINTRE
finds a minimum spanning tree in an undirected graph represented by a distance matrix.

b. Subroutine PMATCH
finds a minimum weight perfect matching in an undirected graph represented by a cost matrix.

c. Subroutine EULER
finds an Euler circuit in an undirected graph represented by a list of edges; the input graph is assumed to be Eulerian.

Since these procedures are of interest by themselves, their parameters will be described in detail.

C. Subroutine TSP Parameters

Input :

N - number of nodes in the complete graph.

NN - equal to $N + \lfloor N / 2 \rfloor$.

NN2 - equal to $(N(N - 1)) / 2$.

DIST - real symmetric matrix of dimension N by N containing the distance for each pair of nodes.

IDIM - row dimension of matrix DIST exactly as specified in the dimension statement of the calling program.

BIG - a sufficiently large real number greater than

$$\sum_{i=1}^{n} \sum_{j=1}^{n} DIST(i,j).$$

EPS - a real number, machine accuracy.

Output :

ISOL - integer vector of length N containing the Hamiltonian circuit.

Working Storages :

WK1 - real vector of length NN2; the input cost matrix, used in the subroutine PMATCH.

WK2 - real vector of length N; used in subroutines MINTRE and PMATCH.

WK3 - real vector of length N; used in subroutine PMATCH.

WK4 - real vector of length N; used in subroutine PMATCH.

WK5 - real vector of length N; used in subroutine PMATCH.

IWK6 - integer vector of length NN; IWK6(i) is one of the end nodes of edge i in the minimum spanning tree, used in subroutines MINTRE and EULER.

IWK7 - integer vector of length NN;
IWK7(i) is one of the end nodes of edge i in the minimum spanning tree, used in subroutines MINTRE and EULER.

IWK8 - integer vector of length NN;
used in subroutines EULER and PMATCH.

IWK9 - integer vector of length NN;
used in subroutines EULER and PMATCH.

IWK10 - integer vector of length NN;
used in subroutines EULER and PMATCH.

IWK11 - integer vector of length N;
set of odd degree nodes in the minimum spanning tree.

IWK12 - integer vector of length N;
used in subroutines EULER and PMATCH.

IWK13 - integer vector of length N;
used in subroutines EULER and PMATCH.

IWK14 - integer vector of length N;
used in subroutines EULER and PMATCH.

IWK15 - integer vector of length N;
used in subroutines EULER, MINTRE and PMATCH.

IWK16 - integer vector of length N;
used in subroutines EULER, MINTRE and PMATCH.

IWK17 - integer vector of length N;
used in subroutine PMATCH.

IWK18 - integer vector of length N;
used in subroutine PMATCH.

Subroutine MINTRE Parameters

Input :

- N - number of nodes in the graph.
- DIST - real symmetric matrix of dimension N by N containing the distance for each pair of nodes.
- IDIM - row dimension of matrix DIST exactly as specified.
- BIG - a sufficiently large real number greater than

$$\sum_{i=1}^{n} \sum_{j=1}^{n} \text{DIST}(i,j).$$

Output :

- INODE, JNODE - each is an integer vector of length N; the two end nodes of edge i in the minimum spanning tree are stored in

  INODE(i), JNODE(i) for i=1,2,...,N-1.

Working Storages :

- WORK - real vector of length N; WORK(i) is the shortest distance from node i to the partial tree being constructed.
- IWORK1 - integer vector of length N; IWORK(i) indicates whether node i has already been included in the minimum spanning tree.
- IWORK2 - integer vector of length N; IWORK2(i) is the father of node i in the minimum spanning tree.

Subroutine PMATCH Parameters

Input :

N - number of nodes in the complete graph; N is assumed to be even.

NN2 - equal to (N(N - 1)) / 2.

COST - real vector of length NN2; the elements in the upper triangular part of the symmetric distance matrix (d_{ij}) of the complete graph are stored columnwise in COST, i.e.,

$$COST(1) = d_{12}, \quad COST(2) = d_{13}, \quad COST(3) = d_{23},$$

$$COST(4) = d_{14}, \quad \ldots, \quad COST(NN2) = d_{N-1,N}.$$

BIG - a sufficiently large real number greater than

$$\sum_{i=1}^{n} \sum_{j=1}^{n} d_{ij} .$$

EPS - a real number, machine precision.

Output :

IPAIR - integer vector of length N containing the minimum weight perfect matching, node i is connected to node IPAIR(i), for i=1,2,...,N.

Working Storages :

WORK1 - real vector of length N.
WORK2 - real vector of length N.
WORK3 - real vector of length N.
WORK4 - real vector of length N.
JWK1 - integer vector of length N.
JWK2 - integer vector of length N.
JWK3 - integer vector of length N.
JWK4 - integer vector of length N.
JWK5 - integer vector of length N.
JWK6 - integer vector of length N.
JWK7 - integer vector of length N.
JWK8 - integer vector of length N.
JWK9 - integer vector of length N.

Subroutine EULER Parameters

Input :

N	-	number of nodes in the graph.
M	-	number of edges in the graph.
INODE, JNODE	-	each is an integer vector of length M; the two end nodes of edge i in the graph are stored in INODE(i), JNODE(i) for i=1,2,...,M; the node and edge numbers of the input graph can be numbered in any order.

Output :

LOOP	-	integer vector of length M containing the Euler circuit.

Working Storages :

IWORK1	-	integer vector of length M; keeps track of the next end node of the arc being traversed.
IWORK2	-	integer vector of length M; IWORK2(i) indicates whether arc i has been visited.
IWORK3	-	integer vector of length N; IWORK3(i) is the number of times that node i is traversed in the Euler circuit.
IWORK4	-	integer vector of length N; the first node of each path to be added to the Euler circuit.
IWORK5	-	integer vector of length N; the last node of each path to be added to the Euler circuit.
IWORK6	-	integer vector of length N; stores the common nodes among cycles which make up the Euler circuit.

D. Test Example

Apply the traveling salesman heuristic algorithm to the complete graph of 15 nodes with the distance matrix given as follows :

```
 0. 29. 82. 46. 68. 52. 72. 42. 51. 55. 29. 74. 23. 72. 46.
29.  0. 55. 46. 42. 43. 43. 23. 23. 31. 41. 51. 11. 52. 21.
82. 55.  0. 68. 46. 55. 23. 43. 41. 29. 79. 21. 64. 31. 51.
46. 46. 68.  0. 82. 15. 72. 31. 62. 42. 21. 51. 51. 43. 64.
68. 42. 46. 82.  0. 74. 23. 52. 21. 46. 82. 58. 46. 65. 23.
52. 43. 55. 15. 74.  0. 61. 23. 55. 31. 33. 37. 51. 29. 59.
72. 43. 23. 72. 23. 61.  0. 42. 23. 31. 77. 37. 51. 46. 33.
42. 23. 43. 31. 52. 23. 42.  0. 33. 15. 37. 33. 33. 31. 37.
51. 23. 41. 62. 21. 55. 23. 33.  0. 29. 62. 46. 29. 51. 11.
55. 31. 29. 42. 46. 31. 31. 15. 29.  0. 51. 21. 41. 23. 37.
29. 41. 79. 21. 82. 33. 77. 37. 62. 51.  0. 65. 42. 59. 61.
74. 51. 21. 51. 58. 37. 37. 33. 46. 21. 65.  0. 61. 11. 55.
23. 11. 64. 51. 46. 51. 51. 33. 29. 41. 42. 61.  0. 62. 23.
72. 52. 31. 43. 65. 29. 46. 31. 51. 23. 59. 11. 62.  0. 59.
46. 21. 51. 64. 23. 59. 33. 37. 11. 37. 61. 55. 23. 59.  0.
```

Main Program

```
      REAL    DIST(15,15),WK1(105),WK2(15),WK3(15),WK4(15),WK5(15)
      INTEGER ISOL(15),IWK6(22),IWK7(22),IWK8(22),IWK9(22),
     +        IWK10(22),IWK11(15),IWK12(15),IWK13(15),IWK14(15),
     +        IWK15(15),IWK16(15),IWK17(15),IWK18(15)
C
      READ(*,10) N
 10   FORMAT(I3)
      DO 20 I = 1, N
 20      READ(*,30) (DIST(I,J),J=1,N)
 30      FORMAT(15F4.0)
      IDIM = 15
      BIG = 1.0E10
      EPS = 1.0E-5
      NN2 = (N * (N - 1)) / 2
      NN = N + (N / 2)
      CALL TSP(N,NN,NN2,DIST,IDIM,BIG,EPS,ISOL,
     +         WK1,WK2,WK3,WK4,WK5,IWK6,IWK7,IWK8,IWK9,IWK10,
     +         IWK11,IWK12,IWK13,IWK14,IWK15,IWK16,IWK17,IWK18)
      WRITE(*,40) (ISOL(I),I=1,N)
 40   FORMAT(/'  THE CIRCUIT FOUND :'//1X,15I4)
      STOP
      END
```

Input Data

```
 15
  0. 29. 82. 46. 68. 52. 72. 42. 51. 55. 29. 74. 23. 72. 46.
 29.  0. 55. 46. 42. 43. 43. 23. 23. 31. 41. 51. 11. 52. 21.
 82. 55.  0. 68. 46. 55. 23. 43. 41. 29. 79. 21. 64. 31. 51.
 46. 46. 68.  0. 82. 15. 72. 31. 62. 42. 21. 51. 51. 43. 64.
 68. 42. 46. 82.  0. 74. 23. 52. 21. 46. 82. 58. 46. 65. 23.
 52. 43. 55. 15. 74.  0. 61. 23. 55. 31. 33. 37. 51. 29. 59.
 72. 43. 23. 72. 23. 61.  0. 42. 23. 31. 77. 37. 51. 46. 33.
 42. 23. 43. 31. 52. 23. 42.  0. 33. 15. 37. 33. 33. 31. 37.
 51. 23. 41. 62. 21. 55. 23. 33.  0. 29. 62. 46. 29. 51. 11.
 55. 31. 29. 42. 46. 31. 31. 15. 29.  0. 51. 21. 41. 23. 37.
 29. 41. 79. 21. 82. 33. 77. 37. 62. 51.  0. 65. 42. 59. 61.
 74. 51. 21. 51. 58. 37. 37. 33. 46. 21. 65.  0. 61. 11. 55.
 23. 11. 64. 51. 46. 51. 51. 33. 29. 41. 42. 61.  0. 62. 23.
 72. 52. 31. 43. 65. 29. 46. 31. 51. 23. 59. 11. 62.  0. 59.
 46. 21. 51. 64. 23. 59. 33. 37. 11. 37. 61. 55. 23. 59.  0.
```

Output Results

```
  THE CIRCUIT FOUND :

    1  13   2  15   9   5   7   3  12  14  10   8   6   4  11
```

```
      SUBROUTINE TSP (N,NN,NN2,DIST,IDIM,BIG,EPS,ISOL,
     +                WK1,WK2,WK3,WK4,WK5,IWK6,IWK7,IWK8,IWK9,IWK10,
     +                IWK11,IWK12,IWK13,IWK14,IWK15,IWK16,IWK17,IWK18)
C
C     Heuristic for the traveling salesman problem
C         satisfying the triangle inequality
C
      REAL    DIST(IDIM,1),WK1(NN2),WK2(N),WK3(N),WK4(N),WK5(N)
      INTEGER ISOL(N),IWK6(NN),IWK7(NN),IWK8(NN),IWK9(NN),
     +        IWK10(NN),IWK11(N),IWK12(N),IWK13(N),IWK14(N),
     +        IWK15(N),IWK16(N),IWK17(N),IWK18(N)
C
C     construct a minimum spanning tree
C
      CALL MINTRE(N,DIST,IDIM,BIG,IWK6,IWK7,WK2,IWK15,IWK16)
C
C     determine the set of nodes with odd degrees in the
C          minimum spanning tree
C
      DO 10 I = 1, N
 10      IWK10(I) = 0
      NM1 = N - 1
      DO 20 I = 1, NM1
         II = IWK6(I)
         JJ = IWK7(I)
         IWK10(II) = IWK10(II) + 1
         IWK10(JJ) = IWK10(JJ) + 1
 20   CONTINUE
      ICT = 0
      DO 30 I = 1, N
         IF (MOD(IWK10(I),2) .NE. 0)  THEN
            ICT = ICT + 1
            IWK11(ICT) = I
         ENDIF
 30   CONTINUE
C
C     determine a minimum weight perfect matching for
C          the set of odd-degree nodes
C
      K = 0
      DO 50 I = 2, ICT
         I1 = I - 1
         DO 40 J = 1, I1
            K = K + 1
            WK1(K) = DIST(IWK11(J),IWK11(I))
 40      CONTINUE
 50   CONTINUE
C
      CALL PMATCH(ICT,NN2,WK1,BIG,EPS,IWK18,WK2,WK3,WK4,WK5,IWK8,
     +            IWK9,IWK10,IWK12,IWK13,IWK14,IWK15,IWK16,IWK17)
C
C     store up the edges in the perfect matching
C
      DO 60 I = 1, ICT
 60      IWK18(I) = IWK11(IWK18(I))
      DO 70 I = 1, N
 70      IWK10(I) = 0
      K = N - 1
      DO 80 I = 1, ICT
         IF (IWK10(IWK11(I)) .EQ. 0)  THEN
            IWK10(IWK11(I)) = 1
            IWK10(IWK18(I)) = 1
            K = K + 1
```

```
            IWK6(K) = IWK11(I)
            IWK7(K) = IWK18(I)
         ENDIF
 80   CONTINUE
C
C     find an Euler circuit
C
      M = N - 1 + (ICT / 2)
      CALL EULER(N,M,IWK6,IWK7,IWK10,IWK8,
     +           IWK9,IWK12,IWK13,IWK14,IWK15)
C
C     form the Hamiltonian circuit
C
      ISOL(1) = IWK10(1)
      J = 2
      ISOL(J) = IWK10(J)
      K = 2
 90   J = J + 1
        IBASE = IWK10(J)
        J1 = J - 1
        DO 100 I = 1, J1
           IF (IBASE .EQ. IWK10(I))  GOTO 90
 100    CONTINUE
        K = K + 1
        ISOL(K) = IWK10(J)
      IF (K .LT. N)  GOTO 90
C
      RETURN
      END
```

```
      SUBROUTINE MINTRE (N,DIST,IDIM,BIG,INODE,JNODE,
     +                   WORK,IWORK1,IWORK2)
C
C     Finding a minimum spanning tree
C       the input graph is represented by a distance matrix
C
      INTEGER INODE(N),JNODE(N),IWORK1(N),IWORK2(N)
      REAL    DIST(IDIM,1),WORK(N)
C
      DO 10 I = 1, N
         WORK(I) = BIG
         IWORK1(I) = 0
         IWORK2(I) = 0
 10   CONTINUE
C
C     find the first non-zero arc
C
      DO 20 IJ = 1, N
         DO 20 KJ = 1, N
            IF (DIST(IJ,KJ) .LT. BIG)  THEN
               I = IJ
               GO TO 30
            ENDIF
 20   CONTINUE
 30   WORK(I) = 0
      IWORK1(I) = 1
      XLEN = 0.
      KK4 = N - 1
      DO 80 JJ = 1, KK4
         DO 40 K = 1, N
 40         WORK(K) = BIG
         DO 60 I = 1, N
C
C           for each forward arc originating at node I calculate
C               the length of the path to node I
C
            IF (IWORK1(I) .EQ. 1)  THEN
               DO 50 J = 1, N
                  IF (DIST(I,J).LT.BIG.AND.IWORK1(J).EQ.0)  THEN
                     D = XLEN + DIST(I,J)
                     IF (D .LT. WORK(J))  THEN
                        WORK(J) = D
                        IWORK2(J) = I
                     ENDIF
                  ENDIF
 50            CONTINUE
            ENDIF
 60      CONTINUE
C
C        find the minimum potential
C
         D = BIG
         IENT = 0
         DO 70 I = 1, N
            IF (IWORK1(I) .EQ. 0 .AND. WORK(I) .LT. D)  THEN
               D = WORK(I)
               IENT = I
               ITR = IWORK2(I)
            ENDIF
 70      CONTINUE
C
C        include the node in the current path
C
```

```
         IF (D .LT. BIG)   THEN
            IWORK1(IENT) = 1
            XLEN = XLEN + DIST(ITR,IENT)
            INODE(JJ) = ITR
            JNODE(JJ) = IENT
         ENDIF
 80   CONTINUE
C
      RETURN
      END
```

```
      SUBROUTINE PMATCH (N,NN2,COST,BIG,EPS,IPAIR,
     +                   WORK1,WORK2,WORK3,WORK4,JWK1,JWK2,
     +                   JWK3,JWK4,JWK5,JWK6,JWK7,JWK8,JWK9)
C
C     Finding a minimum weight perfect matching in a graph
C
      INTEGER IPAIR(N),JWK1(N),JWK2(N),JWK3(N),JWK4(N),JWK5(N),
     +        JWK6(N),JWK7(N),JWK8(N),JWK9(N)
      REAL    COST(NN2),WORK1(N),WORK2(N),WORK3(N),WORK4(N)
C
C     initialization
C
      JWK1(2) = 0
      DO 10 I = 3, N
         JWK1(I) = JWK1(I-1) + I - 2
 10   CONTINUE
      IHEAD = N + 2
      DO 20 I = 1, N
         JWK2(I) = I
         JWK3(I) = I
         JWK4(I) = 0
         JWK5(I) = I
         JWK6(I) = IHEAD
         JWK7(I) = IHEAD
         JWK8(I) = IHEAD
         IPAIR(I) = IHEAD
         WORK1(I) = BIG
         WORK2(I) = 0.
         WORK3(I) = 0.
         WORK4(I) = BIG
 20   CONTINUE
C
C     start procedure
C
      DO 50 I = 1, N
         IF (IPAIR(I) .EQ. IHEAD)  THEN
            NN = 0
            CWK2 = BIG
            DO 40 J = 1, N
               MIN = I
               MAX = J
               IF (I .NE. J)  THEN
                  IF (I .GT. J)  THEN
                     MAX = I
                     MIN = J
                  ENDIF
                  ISUB = JWK1(MAX) + MIN
                  XCST = COST(ISUB)
                  CSWK = COST(ISUB) - WORK2(J)
                  IF (CSWK .LE. CWK2)  THEN
                     IF (CSWK .EQ. CWK2)  THEN
                        IF (NN .EQ. 0) GO TO 30
                        GOTO 40
                     ENDIF
                     CWK2 = CSWK
                     NN = 0
 30                  IF (IPAIR(J) .EQ. IHEAD)  NN = J
                  ENDIF
               ENDIF
 40         CONTINUE
            IF (NN .NE. 0)  THEN
               WORK2(I) = CWK2
               IPAIR(I) = NN
```

```
               IPAIR(NN) = I
            ENDIF
         ENDIF
 50   CONTINUE
C
C     initial labeling
C
      NN = 0
      DO 70 I = 1, N
         IF (IPAIR(I) .EQ. IHEAD)  THEN
            NN = NN + 1
            JWK6(I) = 0
            WORK4(I) = 0.
            XWK2 = WORK2(I)
            DO 60 J = 1, N
               MIN = I
               MAX = J
               IF (I .NE. J)  THEN
                  IF (I .GT. J)  THEN
                     MAX = I
                     MIN = J
                  ENDIF
                  ISUB = JWK1(MAX) + MIN
                  XCST = COST(ISUB)
                  CSWK = COST(ISUB) - XWK2 - WORK2(J)
                  IF (CSWK .LT. WORK1(J))  THEN
                     WORK1(J) = CSWK
                     JWK4(J) = I
                  ENDIF
               ENDIF
 60         CONTINUE
         ENDIF
 70   CONTINUE
      IF (NN .LE. 1) GO TO 340
C
C     examine the labeling and prepare for the next step
C
 80   CSTLOW = BIG
      DO 90 I = 1, N
         IF (JWK2(I) .EQ. I)  THEN
            CST = WORK1(I)
            IF (JWK6(I) .LT. IHEAD)  THEN
               CST = 0.5 * (CST + WORK4(I))
               IF (CST .LE. CSTLOW)  THEN
                  INDEX = I
                  CSTLOW = CST
               ENDIF
            ELSE
               IF (JWK7(I) .LT. IHEAD)  THEN
                  IF (JWK3(I) .NE. I)  THEN
                     CST = CST + WORK2(I)
                     IF (CST .LT. CSTLOW)  THEN
                        INDEX = I
                        CSTLOW = CST
                     ENDIF
                  ENDIF
               ELSE
                  IF (CST .LT. CSTLOW)  THEN
                     INDEX = I
                     CSTLOW = CST
                  ENDIF
               ENDIF
            ENDIF
```

```
         ENDIF
 90   CONTINUE
      IF (JWK7(INDEX) .LT. IHEAD) GO TO 190
      IF (JWK6(INDEX) .LT. IHEAD)  THEN
         LL4 = JWK4(INDEX)
         LL5 = JWK5(INDEX)
         KK4 = INDEX
         KK1 = KK4
         KK5 = JWK2(LL4)
         KK2 = KK5
 100     JWK7(KK1) = KK2
            MM5 = JWK6(KK1)
            IF (MM5 .NE. 0)  THEN
               KK2 = JWK2(MM5)
               KK1 = JWK7(KK2)
               KK1 = JWK2(KK1)
               GO TO 100
            ENDIF
         LL2 = KK1
         KK1 = KK5
         KK2 = KK4
 110     IF (JWK7(KK1) .GE. IHEAD)  THEN
            JWK7(KK1) = KK2
            MM5 = JWK6(KK1)
            IF (MM5 .EQ. 0) GO TO 280
            KK2 = JWK2(MM5)
            KK1 = JWK7(KK2)
            KK1 = JWK2(KK1)
            GO TO 110
         ENDIF
 120     IF (KK1 .EQ. LL2) GO TO 130
            MM5 = JWK7(LL2)
            JWK7(LL2) = IHEAD
            LL1 = IPAIR(MM5)
            LL2 = JWK2(LL1)
            GO TO 120
      ENDIF
C
C     growing an alternating tree, add two edges
C
      JWK7(INDEX) = JWK4(INDEX)
      JWK8(INDEX) = JWK5(INDEX)
      LL1 = IPAIR(INDEX)
      LL3 = JWK2(LL1)
      WORK4(LL3) = CSTLOW
      JWK6(LL3) = IPAIR(LL3)
      CALL SUBB(LL3,N,NN2,BIG,COST,JWK1,JWK2,JWK3,JWK4,
     +          JWK5,JWK7,JWK9,WORK1,WORK2,WORK3,WORK4)
      GO TO 80
C
C     shrink a blossom
C
 130  XWORK = WORK2(LL2) + CSTLOW - WORK4(LL2)
      WORK2(LL2) = 0.
      MM1 = LL2
 140  WORK3(MM1) = WORK3(MM1) + XWORK
         MM1 = JWK3(MM1)
      IF (MM1 .NE. LL2) GO TO 140
         MM5 = JWK3(LL2)
      IF (LL2 .NE. KK5) GO TO 160
 150     KK5 = KK4
         KK2 = JWK7(LL2)
 160  JWK3(MM1) = KK2
```

```
      LL1 = IPAIR(KK2)
      JWK6(KK2) = LL1
      XWK2 = WORK2(KK2) + WORK1(KK2) - CSTLOW
      MM1 = KK2
 170  MM2 = MM1
         WORK3(MM2) = WORK3(MM2) + XWK2
         JWK2(MM2) = LL2
         MM1 = JWK3(MM2)
      IF (MM1 .NE. KK2) GO TO 170
      JWK5(KK2) = MM2
      WORK2(KK2) = XWK2
      KK1 = JWK2(LL1)
      JWK3(MM2) = KK1
      XWK2 = WORK2(KK1) + CSTLOW - WORK4(KK1)
      MM2 = KK1
 180  MM1 = MM2
         WORK3(MM1) = WORK3(MM1) + XWK2
         JWK2(MM1) = LL2
         MM2 = JWK3(MM1)
      IF (MM2 .NE. KK1) GO TO 180
         JWK5(KK1) = MM1
         WORK2(KK1) = XWK2
      IF (KK5 .NE. KK1)  THEN
         KK2 = JWK7(KK1)
         JWK7(KK1) = JWK8(KK2)
         JWK8(KK1) = JWK7(KK2)
         GO TO 160
      ENDIF
      IF (KK5 .NE. INDEX)  THEN
         JWK7(KK5) = LL5
         JWK8(KK5) = LL4
         IF (LL2 .NE. INDEX) GO TO 150
      ELSE
         JWK7(INDEX) = LL4
         JWK8(INDEX) = LL5
      ENDIF
      JWK3(MM1) = MM5
      KK4 = JWK3(LL2)
      JWK4(KK4) = MM5
      WORK4(KK4) = XWORK
      JWK7(LL2) = IHEAD
      WORK4(LL2) = CSTLOW
      CALL SUBB(LL2,N,NN2,BIG,COST,JWK1,JWK2,JWK3,JWK4,
     +          JWK5,JWK7,JWK9,WORK1,WORK2,WORK3,WORK4)
      GO TO 80
C
C     expand a t-labeled blossom
C
 190  KK4 = JWK3(INDEX)
      KK3 = KK4
      LL4 = JWK4(KK4)
      MM2 = KK4
 200  MM1 = MM2
         LL5 = JWK5(MM1)
         XWK2 = WORK2(MM1)
 210     JWK2(MM2) = MM1
         WORK3(MM2) = WORK3(MM2) - XWK2
         IF (MM2 .NE. LL5)  THEN
            MM2 = JWK3(MM2)
            GO TO 210
         ENDIF
         MM2 = JWK3(LL5)
         JWK3(LL5) = MM1
```

```
      IF (MM2 .NE. LL4) GO TO 200
      XWK2 = WORK4(KK4)
      WORK2(INDEX) = XWK2
      JWK3(INDEX) = LL4
      MM2 = LL4
220   WORK3(MM2) = WORK3(MM2) - XWK2
      IF (MM2 .NE. INDEX)  THEN
         MM2 = JWK3(MM2)
         GO TO 220
      ENDIF
      MM1 = IPAIR(INDEX)
      KK1 = JWK2(MM1)
      MM2 = JWK6(KK1)
      LL2 = JWK2(MM2)
      IF (LL2 .NE. INDEX)  THEN
         KK2 = LL2
230      MM5 = JWK7(KK2)
            KK1 = JWK2(MM5)
            IF (KK1 .NE. INDEX)  THEN
               KK2 = JWK6(KK1)
               KK2 = JWK2(KK2)
               GO TO 230
            ENDIF
         JWK7(LL2) = JWK7(INDEX)
         JWK7(INDEX) = JWK8(KK2)
         JWK8(LL2) = JWK8(INDEX)
         JWK8(INDEX) = MM5
         MM3 = JWK6(LL2)
         KK3 = JWK2(MM3)
         MM4 = JWK6(KK3)
         JWK6(LL2) = IHEAD
         IPAIR(LL2) = MM1
         KK1 = KK3
240      MM1 = JWK7(KK1)
            MM2 = JWK8(KK1)
            JWK7(KK1) = MM4
            JWK8(KK1) = MM3
            JWK6(KK1) = MM1
            IPAIR(KK1) = MM1
            KK2 = JWK2(MM1)
            IPAIR(KK2) = MM2
            MM3 = JWK6(KK2)
            JWK6(KK2) = MM2
            IF (KK2 .NE. INDEX)  THEN
               KK1 = JWK2(MM3)
               MM4 = JWK6(KK1)
               JWK7(KK2) = MM3
               JWK8(KK2) = MM4
               GO TO 240
            ENDIF
      ENDIF
      MM2 = JWK8(LL2)
      KK1 = JWK2(MM2)
      WORK1(KK1) = CSTLOW
      KK4 = 0
      IF (KK1 .NE. LL2)  THEN
         MM1 = JWK7(KK1)
         KK3 = JWK2(MM1)
         JWK7(KK1) = JWK7(LL2)
         JWK8(KK1) = MM2
250      MM5 = JWK6(KK1)
            JWK6(KK1) = IHEAD
            KK2 = JWK2(MM5)
```

```
               MM5 = JWK7(KK2)
               JWK7(KK2) = IHEAD
               KK5 = JWK8(KK2)
               JWK8(KK2) = KK4
               KK4 = KK2
               WORK4(KK2) = CSTLOW
               KK1 = JWK2(MM5)
               WORK1(KK1) = CSTLOW
            IF (KK1 .NE. LL2) GO TO 250
            JWK7(LL2) = KK5
            JWK8(LL2) = MM5
            JWK6(LL2) = IHEAD
            IF (KK3 .EQ. LL2) GO TO 270
         ENDIF
         KK1 = 0
         KK2 = KK3
 260     MM5 = JWK6(KK2)
            JWK6(KK2) = IHEAD
            JWK7(KK2) = IHEAD
            JWK8(KK2) = KK1
            KK1 = JWK2(MM5)
            MM5 = JWK7(KK1)
            JWK6(KK1) = IHEAD
            JWK7(KK1) = IHEAD
            JWK8(KK1) = KK2
            KK2 = JWK2(MM5)
         IF (KK2 .NE. LL2) GO TO 260
         CALL SUBA(KK1,N,NN2,BIG,COST,JWK1,JWK2,JWK3,JWK4,
     +             JWK5,JWK6,JWK8,WORK1,WORK2,WORK3,WORK4)
C
 270     IF (KK4 .EQ. 0) GO TO 80
            LL2 = KK4
            CALL SUBB(LL2,N,NN2,BIG,COST,JWK1,JWK2,JWK3,JWK4,
     +                JWK5,JWK7,JWK9,WORK1,WORK2,WORK3,WORK4)
            KK4 = JWK8(LL2)
            JWK8(LL2) = IHEAD
            GO TO 270
C
C        augmentation of the matching
C        exchange the matching and non-matching edges along the
C           augmenting path
C
 280     LL2 = KK4
         MM5 = LL4
 290     KK1 = LL2
 300        IPAIR(KK1) = MM5
            MM5 = JWK6(KK1)
            JWK7(KK1) = IHEAD
            IF (MM5 .NE. 0)  THEN
               KK2 = JWK2(MM5)
               MM1 = JWK7(KK2)
               MM5 = JWK8(KK2)
               KK1 = JWK2(MM1)
               IPAIR(KK2) = MM1
               GO TO 300
            ENDIF
            IF (LL2 .EQ. KK4)  THEN
               LL2 = KK5
               MM5 = LL5
               GO TO 290
            ENDIF
C
```

```
C     remove all labels of non-exposed base nodes
C
      DO 310 I = 1, N
         IF (JWK2(I) .EQ. I)  THEN
            IF (JWK6(I) .LT. IHEAD)  THEN
               CST = CSTLOW - WORK4(I)
               WORK2(I) = WORK2(I) + CST
               JWK6(I) = IHEAD
               IF (IPAIR(I) .NE. IHEAD)  THEN
                  WORK4(I) = BIG
               ELSE
                  JWK6(I) = 0
                  WORK4(I) = 0.
               ENDIF
            ELSE
               IF (JWK7(I) .LT. IHEAD)  THEN
                  CST = WORK1(I) - CSTLOW
                  WORK2(I) = WORK2(I) + CST
                  JWK7(I) = IHEAD
                  JWK8(I) = IHEAD
               ENDIF
               WORK4(I) = BIG
            ENDIF
            WORK1(I) = BIG
         ENDIF
 310  CONTINUE
      NN = NN - 2
      IF (NN .LE. 1) GO TO 340
C
C     determine the new WORK1 values
C
      DO 330 I = 1, N
         KK1 = JWK2(I)
         IF (JWK6(KK1) .EQ. 0)  THEN
            XWK2 = WORK2(KK1)
            XWK3 = WORK3(I)
            DO 320 J = 1, N
               KK2 = JWK2(J)
               IF (KK1 .NE. KK2)  THEN
                  MIN = I
                  MAX = J
                  IF (I .NE. J)  THEN
                     IF (I .GT. J)  THEN
                        MAX = I
                        MIN = J
                     ENDIF
                     ISUB = JWK1(MAX) + MIN
                     XCST = COST(ISUB)
                     CSWK = COST(ISUB) - XWK2 - XWK3
                     CSWK = CSWK - WORK2(KK2) - WORK3(J)
                     IF (CSWK .LT. WORK1(KK2))  THEN
                        JWK4(KK2) = I
                        JWK5(KK2) = J
                        WORK1(KK2) = CSWK
                     ENDIF
                  ENDIF
               ENDIF
 320        CONTINUE
         ENDIF
 330  CONTINUE
      GO TO 80
C
```

```
C     generate the original graph by expanding all shrunken blossoms
C
 340  VALUE = 0.
      DO 350 I = 1, N
         IF (JWK2(I) .EQ. I)  THEN
            IF (JWK6(I) .GE. 0)  THEN
               KK5 = IPAIR(I)
               KK2 = JWK2(KK5)
               KK4 = IPAIR(KK2)
               JWK6(I) = -1
               JWK6(KK2) = -1
               MIN = KK4
               MAX = KK5
               IF (KK4 .NE. KK5)  THEN
                  IF (KK4 .GT. KK5)  THEN
                     MAX = KK4
                     MIN = KK5
                  ENDIF
                  ISUB = JWK1(MAX) + MIN
                  XCST = COST(ISUB)
                  VALUE = VALUE + XCST
               ENDIF
            ENDIF
         ENDIF
 350  CONTINUE
      DO 420 I = 1, N
 360     LL2 = JWK2(I)
         IF (LL2 .EQ. I) GO TO 420
         MM2 = JWK3(LL2)
         LL4 = JWK4(MM2)
         KK3 = MM2
         XWORK = WORK4(MM2)
 370     MM1 = MM2
            LL5 = JWK5(MM1)
            XWK2 = WORK2(MM1)
 380        JWK2(MM2) = MM1
            WORK3(MM2) = WORK3(MM2) - XWK2
            IF (MM2 .NE. LL5)  THEN
               MM2 = JWK3(MM2)
               GO TO 380
            ENDIF
            MM2 = JWK3(LL5)
            JWK3(LL5) = MM1
         IF (MM2 .NE. LL4) GO TO 370
         WORK2(LL2) = XWORK
         JWK3(LL2) = LL4
         MM2 = LL4
 390     WORK3(MM2) = WORK3(MM2) - XWORK
         IF (MM2 .NE. LL2)  THEN
            MM2 = JWK3(MM2)
            GO TO 390
         ENDIF
         MM5 = IPAIR(LL2)
         MM1 = JWK2(MM5)
         MM1 = IPAIR(MM1)
         KK1 = JWK2(MM1)
         IF (LL2 .NE. KK1)  THEN
            IPAIR(KK1) = MM5
            KK3 = JWK7(KK1)
            KK3 = JWK2(KK3)
 400        MM3 = JWK6(KK1)
               KK2 = JWK2(MM3)
               MM1 = JWK7(KK2)
```

```
               MM2 = JWK8(KK2)
               KK1 = JWK2(MM1)
               IPAIR(KK1) = MM2
               IPAIR(KK2) = MM1
               MIN = MM1
               MAX = MM2
               IF (MM1 .EQ. MM2)  GOTO 360
               IF (MM1 .GT. MM2)  THEN
                  MAX = MM1
                  MIN = MM2
               ENDIF
               ISUB = JWK1(MAX) + MIN
               XCST = COST(ISUB)
               VALUE = VALUE + XCST
            IF (KK1 .NE. LL2) GO TO 400
            IF (KK3 .EQ. LL2) GO TO 360
         ENDIF
 410     KK5 = JWK6(KK3)
            KK2 = JWK2(KK5)
            KK6 = JWK6(KK2)
            MIN = KK5
            MAX = KK6
            IF (KK5 .EQ. KK6)  GOTO 360
            IF (KK5 .GT. KK6)  THEN
               MAX = KK5
               MIN = KK6
            ENDIF
            ISUB = JWK1(MAX) + MIN
            XCST = COST(ISUB)
            VALUE = VALUE + XCST
            KK6 = JWK7(KK2)
            KK3 = JWK2(KK6)
            IF (KK3 .EQ. LL2) GO TO 360
         GO TO 410
 420  CONTINUE
C
      RETURN
      END
```

```
      SUBROUTINE SUBA (KK,N,NN2,BIG,COST,JWK1,JWK2,JWK3,JWK4,
     +                 JWK5,JWK6,JWK8,WORK1,WORK2,WORK3,WORK4)
C
C     This subprogram is used by subroutine PMATCH
C
      INTEGER JWK1(N),JWK2(N),JWK3(N),JWK4(N),JWK5(N),JWK6(N),
     +        JWK8(N)
      REAL    COST(NN2),WORK1(N),WORK2(N),WORK3(N),WORK4(N)
C
      IHEAD = N + 2
 10   JJ1 = KK
      KK = JWK8(JJ1)
      JWK8(JJ1) = IHEAD
      CSTWK = BIG
      JJ3 = 0
      JJ4 = 0
      J = JJ1
      XWK2 = WORK2(JJ1)
 20   XWK3 = WORK3(J)
      DO 30 I = 1, N
         JJ2 = JWK2(I)
         IF (JWK6(JJ2) .LT. IHEAD)  THEN
            MIN = J
            MAX = I
            IF (J .NE. I)  THEN
               IF (J .GT. I)  THEN
                  MAX = J
                  MIN = I
               ENDIF
               ISUB = JWK1(MAX) + MIN
               XCST = COST(ISUB)
               CSWK = COST(ISUB) - XWK2 - XWK3
               CSWK = CSWK - WORK2(JJ2) - WORK3(I)
               CSWK = CSWK + WORK4(JJ2)
               IF (CSWK .LT. CSTWK)  THEN
                  JJ3 = I
                  JJ4 = J
                  CSTWK = CSWK
               ENDIF
            ENDIF
         ENDIF
 30   CONTINUE
      J = JWK3(J)
      IF (J .NE. JJ1) GO TO 20
      JWK4(JJ1) = JJ3
      JWK5(JJ1) = JJ4
      WORK1(JJ1) = CSTWK
      IF (KK .NE. 0) GO TO 10
C
      RETURN
      END
```

```
      SUBROUTINE SUBB (KK,N,NN2,BIG,COST,JWK1,JWK2,JWK3,JWK4,
     +                 JWK5,JWK7,JWK9,WORK1,WORK2,WORK3,WORK4)
C
C     This subprogram is used by subroutine PMATCH
C
      INTEGER JWK1(N),JWK2(N),JWK3(N),JWK4(N),JWK5(N),
     +        JWK7(N),JWK9(N)
      REAL    COST(NN2),WORK1(N),WORK2(N),WORK3(N),WORK4(N)
C
      IHEAD = N + 2
      XWK1 = WORK4(KK) - WORK2(KK)
      WORK1(KK) = BIG
      XWK2 = XWK1 - WORK3(KK)
      JWK7(KK) = 0
      II = 0
      DO 10 I = 1, N
         JJ3 = JWK2(I)
         IF (JWK7(JJ3) .GE. IHEAD)  THEN
            II = II + 1
            JWK9(II) = I
            MIN = KK
            MAX = I
            IF (KK .NE. I)  THEN
               IF (KK .GT. I)  THEN
                  MAX = KK
                  MIN = I
               ENDIF
               ISUB = JWK1(MAX) + MIN
               CSWK = COST(ISUB) + XWK2
               CSWK = CSWK - WORK2(JJ3) - WORK3(I)
               IF (CSWK .LT. WORK1(JJ3))  THEN
                  JWK4(JJ3) = KK
                  JWK5(JJ3) = I
                  WORK1(JJ3) = CSWK
               ENDIF
            ENDIF
         ENDIF
   10 CONTINUE
      JWK7(KK) = IHEAD
      JJ1 = KK
      JJ1 = JWK3(JJ1)
      IF (JJ1 .EQ. KK)  RETURN
   20 XWK2 = XWK1 - WORK3(JJ1)
      DO 30 I = 1, II
         JJ2 = JWK9(I)
         JJ3 = JWK2(JJ2)
         MIN = JJ1
         MAX = JJ2
         IF (JJ1 .NE. JJ2)  THEN
            IF (JJ1 .GT. JJ2)  THEN
               MAX = JJ1
               MIN = JJ2
            ENDIF
            ISUB = JWK1(MAX) + MIN
            XCST = COST(ISUB)
            CSWK = COST(ISUB) + XWK2
            CSWK = CSWK - WORK2(JJ3) - WORK3(JJ2)
            IF (CSWK .LT. WORK1(JJ3))  THEN
               JWK4(JJ3) = JJ1
               JWK5(JJ3) = JJ2
               WORK1(JJ3) = CSWK
            ENDIF
         ENDIF
```

```
 30   CONTINUE
      JJ1 = JWK3(JJ1)
      IF (JJ1 .NE. KK) GO TO 20
C
      RETURN
      END
```

```
      SUBROUTINE EULER (N,M,INODE,JNODE,LOOP,
     +                  IWORK1,IWORK2,IWORK3,IWORK4,IWORK5,IWORK6)
C
C     Finding an Euler circuit in an Eulerian graph
C
      INTEGER INODE(M),JNODE(M),LOOP(M),IWORK1(M),IWORK2(M),
     +        IWORK3(N),IWORK4(N),IWORK5(N),IWORK6(N)
      LOGICAL FOUND,COPYON
C
      DO 10 I = 1, N
 10      IWORK3(I) = 0
      DO 20 I = 1, M
         LOOP(I) = 0
         IWORK1(I) = 0
 20      IWORK2(I) = 0
      NUMARC = 1
      IWORK2(1) = 1
      NNODE = 1
      I = INODE(1)
      IWORK1(NNODE) = I
      IWORK3(I) = 1
      NNODE = NNODE + 1
      J = JNODE(1)
      IWORK1(NNODE) = J
      IWORK3(J) = 1
      IBASE = J
      NBREAK = 0
C
C     look for the next arc
C
 30   DO 40 I = 2, M
         IF (IWORK2(I) .EQ. 0)  THEN
            FOUND = .FALSE.
            IF (IBASE .EQ. INODE(I))  THEN
               FOUND = .TRUE.
               IBASE = JNODE(I)
            ELSE
               IF (IBASE .EQ. JNODE(I))  THEN
                  FOUND = .TRUE.
                  IBASE = INODE(I)
               ENDIF
            ENDIF
            IF (FOUND)  THEN
               IWORK2(I) = 1
               NUMARC = NUMARC + 1
               NNODE = NNODE + 1
               IF (NNODE .LE. M)  IWORK1(NNODE) = IBASE
               IWORK3(IBASE) = 1
               GOTO 30
            ENDIF
         ENDIF
 40   CONTINUE
C
C     a cycle has been found
C
      IF (NBREAK .GT. 0)  THEN
         NNODE = NNODE - 1
         IWORK5(NBREAK) = NNODE
      ENDIF
      IF (NUMARC  .LT.  M)  THEN
C
C     find a node in the current Euler circuit
C
```

```
         DO 50 I = 2, M
            IF (IWORK2(I) .EQ. 0)  THEN
               FOUND = .FALSE.
               IF (IWORK3(INODE(I)) .NE. 0)  THEN
                  FOUND = .TRUE.
                  J = INODE(I)
                  K = JNODE(I)
               ELSE
                  IF (IWORK3(JNODE(I)) .NE. 0)  THEN
                     FOUND = .TRUE.
                     J = JNODE(I)
                     K = INODE(I)
                  ENDIF
               ENDIF
C
C              identify a path which will be added to the circuit
C
               IF (FOUND)  THEN
                  NBREAK = NBREAK + 1
                  IWORK6(NBREAK) = J
                  IBASE = K
                  IWORK3(K) = 1
                  NNODE = NNODE + 1
                  IWORK4(NBREAK) = NNODE
                  IWORK1(NNODE) = IBASE
                  IWORK2(I) = 1
                  NUMARC = NUMARC + 1
                  GOTO 30
               ENDIF
            ENDIF
 50      CONTINUE
      ENDIF
C
C     form the Euler circuit
C
      IF (NBREAK .EQ. 0)  THEN
         NNODE = NNODE - 1
         DO 60 I = 1, NNODE
 60         LOOP(I) = IWORK1(I)
         RETURN
      ENDIF
      INSERT = 1
      IPIVOT = IWORK6(INSERT)
      IFORWD = 0
 70   NCOPY = 1
      IBASE = IWORK1(1)
      LOCBAS = 1
      LOOP(NCOPY) = IBASE
C
C     a path identified before is added to the circuit
C
 80   IF (IBASE .EQ. IPIVOT)  THEN
         J = IWORK4(INSERT) + IFORWD
         K = IWORK5(INSERT) + IFORWD
         DO 90 L = J, K
            NCOPY = NCOPY + 1
            LOOP(NCOPY) = IWORK1(L)
            IWORK1(L) = 0
 90      CONTINUE
         NCOPY = NCOPY + 1
C
C        add the intersecting node to the circuit
C
```

```
         LOOP(NCOPY) = IBASE
         IFORWD = IFORWD + 1
         IF (NCOPY .LT. NNODE)  THEN
 100        IF (NCOPY .LT. M)  THEN
               LOCBAS = LOCBAS + 1
               IF (LOCBAS .LT. M)  THEN
                  IBASE = IWORK1(LOCBAS)
                  IF (IBASE .NE. 0)  THEN
                     NCOPY = NCOPY + 1
                     LOOP(NCOPY) = IBASE
                  ENDIF
                  GOTO 100
               ENDIF
            ENDIF
         ENDIF
      ELSE
         NCOPY = NCOPY + 1
         IF (NCOPY .LE. NNODE)  THEN
            LOCBAS = LOCBAS + 1
            IBASE = IWORK1(LOCBAS)
            LOOP(NCOPY) = IBASE
            GOTO 80
         ENDIF
      ENDIF
C
C     check if more paths are to be added to the circuit
C
      COPYON = .FALSE.
      INSERT = INSERT + 1
      IF (INSERT .LE. NBREAK)  THEN
         COPYON = .TRUE.
         IPIVOT = IWORK6(INSERT)
      ENDIF
      IF (COPYON)  THEN
         DO 110 I = 1, M
C           IF (LOOP(I) .NE. 0)  IWORK1(I) = LOOP(I)
C           LOOP(I) = 0
            IWORK1(I) = LOOP(I)
 110     CONTINUE
         GOTO 70
      ENDIF
C
      RETURN
      END
```

Chapter 5

STEINER TREE PROBLEM

A. Problem Description

Consider an undirected graph G, each of its edges is labeled with a distance. Let S be a specified subset of nodes of G. The *Steiner tree problem* is to find a tree of G that spans S with minimal total distance on its edges. The nodes in the set S are called *Steiner points.*

Let n be the number of nodes in G, p be the number of Steiner points, and k be the number of leaves in the optimal Steiner tree. The heuristic algorithm to be described will find a solution with total distance no more than

$$2 (1 - 1/k)$$

times that of the optimal tree in time $O(pn^2)$.

B. Algorithm

Step 1. Construct the complete undirected graph H from G and S in such a way that

the set of nodes in H is equal to S;
for every edge (u,v) in H, the
distance of (u,v) is set equal to
the distance of the shortest path
between node u and node v in G.

Step 2. Find a minimum spanning tree T_H of H.

Step 3. Replace each edge (u,v) in T_H by a shortest path between node u and node v in G;
the resulting graph R is a subgraph of G.

Step 4. Find a minimum spanning tree T_R of R.

Step 5. Delete edges in T_R, if necessary, so that all the leaves in T_R are elements of S. The resulting tree is returned as the solution.

Remarks

To estimate how close the heuristic solution comes to an optimal one, let T_{opt} be the optimal Steiner tree, k be the total number of leaves in T_{opt}. Denote the total distance on the edges of T_{opt} by Z_{opt}, and the total distance on the edges of the Steiner tree computed by the above heuristic algorithm by Z_h. If an edge is added in parallel to every edge in T_{opt}, then there is an Euler circuit C in T_{opt}. The circuit C can be regarded as composed of k simple paths, each connecting a leaf to another leaf. By deleting from C the longest simple path, a walk W can be constructed such that the total distance of W is no more than

$$(1 - 1/k) * \text{total distance of } C$$

which is equal to

$$2\ (1 - 1/k)\ Z_{opt}.$$

On the other hand, the total distance of W is greater than the total distance on the edges of T_H. Hence

$$Z_h \le 2\ (1 - 1/k)\ Z_{opt}\ .$$

Note that subroutine STREE calls on two auxiliary procedures :

a. Subroutine SHORTP
   finds a shortest path between two nodes in an undirected graph represented by a list of edges.

b. Subroutine MSPTRE
   finds a minimum spanning tree in an undirected graph represented by a list of edges.

Since these procedures are of interest by themselves, their parameters will be described in detail.

C. Subroutine STREE Parameters

Input :

N - number of nodes in the graph.

M - number of edges in the graph.

INODE, JNODE - each is an integer vector of length M; the two end nodes of edge i in the graph are stored in

INODE(i), JNODE(i) for i=1,2,...,M;

the node and edge numbers of the input graph can be numbered in any order.

ARCOST - real vector of length M; the edge distance of edge i is stored in

ARCOST(i), i-1,2,...,M.

NS - number of Steiner points.

SPOINT - boolean vector of length N; SPOINT(i) has the value TRUE if node i is a Steiner point, otherwise SPOINT(i) has the value FALSE.

BIG - a sufficiently large real number greater than

$$\sum_{i=1}^{M} \text{ARCOST}(i) .$$

Output :

NSP - number of edges in the Steiner tree found by the subroutine.

ISTREE, JSTREE - each is an integer vector of length N; the two end nodes of edge i in the Steiner tree are stored in

ISTREE(i), JSTREE(i) for i=1,2,...,NSP.

XLEN - the total length of edges in the Steiner tree.

Working Storages :

IWK1 - integer vector of length N; IWK1(i) is the end node of arc i in the minimum spanning tree, used in subroutine MSPTRE.

IWK2 - integer vector of length N; IWK2(i) is the other end node of arc i in the minimum spanning tree, used in subroutine MSPTRE.

IWK3 - boolean vector of length N;
IWK3(i) indicates whether node i has already been included into the structure being constructed, used in subroutines MSPTRE and SHORTP.

IWK4 - integer vector of length N;
stores the shortest path, used in subroutine SHORTP.

IWK5 - integer vector of length N;
IWK5(i) is the index of node i being considered, used in subroutine SHORTP.

IWK6 - integer vector of length N;
pointer to the original arc list, used in subroutine MSPTRE.

IWK7 - integer vector of length N;
IWK7(i) is the father of node i, used in subroutine MSPTRE.

IWK8 - integer vector of length M;
IWK8(i) is the end node of arc i being considered, used in subroutine MSPTRE.

IWK9 - integer vector of length M;
IWK9(i) is the pointer to arc i, used in subroutine MSPTRE.

IWK10 - integer vector of length M;
IWK10(i) is the end node of arc i being considered.

IWK11 - integer vector of length M;
IWK11(i) is the other end node of arc i.

IWK12 - integer vector of length NS;
IWK12(i) is the original node index of Steiner point i.

WORK13 - real vector of length N;
WORK13(i) is the shortest distance from node i to the structure being constructed, used in subroutines MSPTRE and SHORTP.

WORK14 - real vector of length M;
WORK14(i) is the cost of arc i in the complete graph of Steiner points.

Subroutine SHORTP Parameters

Input :

N - number of nodes in the graph.

M - number of edges in the graph.

INODE, JNODE - each is an integer vector of length M; the two end nodes of edge i in the graph are stored in

INODE(i), JNODE(i) for i=1,2,...,M;

the node and edge numbers of the input graph can be numbered in any order.

ARCOST - real vector of length M; the edge distance of edge i is stored in

ARCOST(i), i=1,2,...,M.

ISTART, LAST - a shortest path between node ISTART and node LAST is to be found.

BIG - a sufficiently large real number greater than

$$\sum_{i=1}^{M} \text{ARCOST}(i).$$

Output :

NUMP - the number of nodes in the shortest path found between ISTART and LAST (including ISTART and LAST).

ISPATH - integer vector of length N; the shortest path between ISTART and LAST is in

ISPATH(i), ISPATH(2), ..., ISPATH(NUMP).

XLEN - total length of the shortest path between ISTART and LAST.

NP - the integer NP has the value zero if a shortest path is found between ISTART and LAST, otherwise it has the value one.

Working Storages :

IWORK1 - boolean vector of length N; IWORK1(i) indicates whether node i has been labeled.

IWORK2 - integer vector of length N;
IWORK2(i) is the index of node i being considered.

IWORK3 - integer vector of length M;
IWORK3(i) is the original arc index of arc i being considered.

WK4 - real vector of length N;
WK4(i) is the shortest distance from node i to the shortest path being constructed.

Subroutine MSPTRE Parameters

Input :

N - number of nodes in the graph.

M - number of edges in the graph.

INODE, JNODE - each is an integer vector of length M;
the two end nodes of edge i in the graph are stored in
INODE(i), JNODE(i) for i=1,2,...,M;
the node and edge numbers of the input graph can be numbered in any order.

ARCOST - real vector of length M;
the edge distance of edge i is stored in
ARCOST(i), i=1,2,...,M.

BIG - a sufficiently large real number greater than

$$\sum_{i=1}^{M} \text{ARCOST}(i).$$

Output :

ITREE, JTREE - each is an integer vector of length N;
edges of the minimum spanning tree are stored in
ITREE(i), JTREE(i) for i=1,2,...,N-1.

XLEN - total length of the edges in the minimum spanning tree.

Working Storages :

IWORK1 - integer vector of length N;
IWORK1(i) is the father of node i in the minimum spanning tree.

IWORK2 - integer vector of length N;
pointer vector of the original arc list.

IWORK3 - boolean vector of length N;
IWORK3(i) indicates whether node i has already been included in the minimum spanning tree.

IWORK4 - integer vector of length M;
IWORK4(i) is the end node of arc i being considered.

IWORK5 - integer vector of length M;
IWORK5(i) is the index of arc i.

WK6 - real vector of length N;
WK6(i) is the shortest distance from node i to the partial tree being constructed.

D. Test Example

Consider an undirected graph of 10 nodes and 20 edges. The edge distances are given as follows :

edge number	two end nodes		edge distance
1	2	1	6.0
2	3	2	2.0
3	8	3	6.0
4	10	6	9.0
5	4	2	3.0
6	3	4	4.0
7	7	3	5.0
8	8	7	9.0
9	9	8	3.0
10	10	9	4.0
11	4	1	3.0
12	7	4	2.0
13	9	7	3.0
14	5	1	5.0
15	10	5	8.0
16	5	4	6.0
17	7	5	7.0
18	5	6	4.0
19	7	6	4.0
20	9	6	8.0

The Steiner points are 1, 3, 6, 9, 10.

Main Program

```
      INTEGER INODE(20),JNODE(20),ISTREE(10),JSTREE(10),
     +        IWK1(10),IWK2(10),IWK4(10),IWK5(10),IWK6(10),
     +        IWK7(10),IWK8(20),IWK9(20),IWK10(20),
     +        IWK11(20),IWK12(5)
      REAL    ARCOST(20),WORK13(10),WORK14(20)
      LOGICAL SPOINT(10),IWK3(10)
C
      READ(*,10) N,M,NS
 10   FORMAT(3I3)
C
      DO 20 I = 1, M
 20      READ(*,30) INODE(I),JNODE(I),ARCOST(I)
 30      FORMAT(2I3,F6.0)
C
      DO 40 I = 1, N
 40      SPOINT(I) = .FALSE.
C
      DO 60 I = 1, NS
         READ(*,50) NSTEIN
 50      FORMAT(I3)
 60      SPOINT(NSTEIN) = .TRUE.
C
      BIG = 1.0E10
C
      CALL STREE(N,M,INODE,JNODE,ARCOST,NS,SPOINT,BIG,NSP,
     +           ISTREE,JSTREE,XLEN,IWK1,IWK2,IWK3,IWK4,
     +           IWK5,IWK6,IWK7,IWK8,IWK9,IWK10,IWK11,
     +           IWK12,WORK13,WORK14)
C
      WRITE(*,70)
 70   FORMAT(/'  THE STEINER TREE EDGES:'/)
      DO 80 I = 1, NSP
 80      WRITE(*,90) ISTREE(I),JSTREE(I)
 90      FORMAT(5X,'(',I2,',',I3,' )')
      WRITE(*,100) XLEN
 100  FORMAT(/'  TOTAL LENGTH =',F10.1)
C
      STOP
      END
```

Input Data

```
10 20  5
 2  1  6.0
 3  2  2.0
 8  3  6.0
10  6  9.0
 4  2  3.0
 3  4  4.0
 7  3  5.0
 8  7  9.0
 9  8  3.0
10  9  4.0
 4  1  3.0
 7  4  2.0
 9  7  3.0
 5  1  5.0
10  5  8.0
 5  4  6.0
 7  5  7.0
 5  6  4.0
 7  6  4.0
 9  6  8.0
 3
 1
10
 6
 9
```

Output Results

```
THE STEINER TREE EDGES:

    ( 3,  4 )
    ( 4,  7 )
    ( 4,  1 )
    ( 7,  9 )
    ( 7,  6 )
    ( 9, 10 )

TOTAL LENGTH =       20.0
```

```
      SUBROUTINE STREE (N,M,INODE,JNODE,ARCOST,NS,SPOINT,BIG,NSP,
     +                  ISTREE,JSTREE,XLEN,IWK1,IWK2,IWK3,IWK4,
     +                  IWK5,IWK6,IWK7,IWK8,IWK9,IWK10,IWK11,
     +                  IWK12,WORK13,WORK14)
C
C     Minimal Steiner tree heuristic
C
      INTEGER INODE(M),JNODE(M),ISTREE(N),JSTREE(N),IWK1(N),
     +        IWK2(N),IWK4(N),IWK5(N),IWK6(N),IWK7(N),IWK8(M),
     +        IWK9(M),IWK10(M),IWK11(M),IWK12(NS)
      REAL    ARCOST(M),WORK13(N),WORK14(M)
      LOGICAL SPOINT(N),IWK3(N)
C
C       identify the Steiner points
C
       IT = 0
       DO 10 I = 1, N
          IF (SPOINT(I)) THEN
             IT = IT + 1
             IWK12(IT) = I
          ENDIF
 10    CONTINUE
C
C       construct the complete graph for the Steiner points
C
       IL = 0
       II = 2
       NNS1 = NS - 1
       DO 30 I = 1, NNS1
          DO 20 J = II, NS
             IF (I .NE. J) THEN
                IL = IL + 1
                IWK10(IL) = IWK12(I)
                IWK11(IL) = IWK12(J)
                CALL SHORTP(N,M,INODE,JNODE,ARCOST,IWK12(I),
     +                      IWK12(J),BIG,NUMP,IWK4,XLEN,NP,IWK3,
     +                      IWK5,IWK9,WORK13)
                WORK14(IL) = XLEN
             ENDIF
 20       CONTINUE
          II = II + 1
 30    CONTINUE
       LL = (NS * (NS - 1)) / 2
       MX = 0
       DO 40 I = 1, IT
          IF (IWK12(I) .GT. MX)  MX = IWK12(I)
 40    CONTINUE
C
C       find a minimum spanning tree of the complete graph
C
       CALL MSPTRE(MX,LL,IWK10,IWK11,WORK14,BIG,IWK1,IWK2,
     +             XLEN,IWK7,IWK6,IWK3,IWK8,IWK9,WORK13)
       DO 50 I = 1, M
 50       IWK10(I) = 0
C
C       construct the subgraph by replacing each edge of the
C       minimum spanning tree by its corresponding shortest path
C
       DO 80 I = 1, NNS1
          II = IWK1(I)
          JJ = IWK2(I)
          CALL SHORTP(N,M,INODE,JNODE,ARCOST,II,JJ,BIG,NUMP,
     +                IWK4,XLEN,NP,IWK3,IWK5,IWK9,WORK13)
```

```
         NUMP1 = NUMP - 1
         DO 70 IJ = 1, NUMP1
            IV1 = IWK4(IJ)
            IV2 = IWK4(IJ+1)
            DO 60 JK = 1, M
               IF ((INODE(JK).EQ.IV1 .AND. JNODE(JK).EQ.IV2) .OR.
     +             (INODE(JK).EQ.IV2 .AND. JNODE(JK).EQ.IV1))
     +              KK1 = JK
 60         CONTINUE
            IWK10(KK1) = -1
 70      CONTINUE
 80   CONTINUE
      DO 90 I = 1, M
         IF (IWK10(I) .EQ. 0) THEN
            INODE(I) = 0
            JNODE(I) = 0
         ENDIF
 90   CONTINUE
C
C     find a minimum spanning tree of the subgraph
C
      CALL MSPTRE(N,M,INODE,JNODE,ARCOST,BIG,IWK1,IWK2,
     +            XLEN,IWK7,IWK6,IWK3,IWK8,IWK9,WORK13)
      IN = 0
      DO 100 I = 1, N
         IF (IWK1(I) .NE. 0) IN = IN + 1
 100  CONTINUE
C
C     construct a Steiner tree by deleting edges, if necessary,
C        such that all leaves are Steiner points
C
      DO 160 J = 1, IN
         IFLAG = 0
         DO 150 I = 1, IN
            IF (IWK1(I) .NE. 0 .AND. IWK2(I) .NE. 0) THEN
               L = IWK2(I)
               IC1 = 0
               DO 110 K = 1, IN
                  IF (IWK1(K) .EQ. L) THEN
                     IC1 = IC1 + 1
                     IWK9(IC1) = K
                     IWK8(IC1) = IWK2(K)
                  ENDIF
                  IF (IWK2(K) .EQ. L) THEN
                     IC1 = IC1 + 1
                     IWK9(IC1) = K
                     IWK8(IC1) = IWK1(K)
                  ENDIF
 110           CONTINUE
               L = IWK1(I)
               IC2 = 0
               DO 120 K = 1, IN
                  IF (IWK1(K) .EQ. L) THEN
                     IC2 = IC2 + 1
                     IWK9(IC2) = K
                     IWK8(IC2) = IWK2(K)
                  ENDIF
                  IF (IWK2(K) .EQ. L) THEN
                     IC2 = IC2 + 1
                     IWK9(IC2) = K
                     IWK8(IC2) = IWK1(K)
                  ENDIF
 120           CONTINUE
```

```
             II = IWK1(I)
             JJ = IWK2(I)
             IF ((IC1 .EQ. 1 .AND. (.NOT. SPOINT(JJ))) .OR.
     +          (IC2 .EQ. 1 .AND. (.NOT. SPOINT(II)))) THEN
                DO 130 K = 1, M
                   IF (INODE(K) .EQ. IWK1(I) .AND.
     +                 JNODE(K) .EQ. IWK2(I)) THEN
                      KK = K
                      GO TO 140
                   ENDIF
 130            CONTINUE
 140            IWK1(I) = 0
                IWK2(I) = 0
                IFLAG = 1
                XLEN = XLEN - ARCOST(KK)
             ENDIF
          ENDIF
 150     CONTINUE
         IF (IFLAG .EQ. 0) GO TO 170
 160  CONTINUE
C
C     store the solution
C
 170  I = 0
      DO 180 J = 1, IN
         IF (IWK1(J) .NE. 0 .AND. IWK2(J) .NE. 0) THEN
            I = I + 1
            ISTREE(I) = IWK1(J)
            JSTREE(I) = IWK2(J)
         ENDIF
 180  CONTINUE
      NSP = I
C
      RETURN
      END
```

```
      SUBROUTINE SHORTP (N,M,INODE,JNODE,ARCOST,ISTART,LAST,BIG,NUMP,
     +                   ISPATH,XLEN,NP,IWORK1,IWORK2,IWORK3,WK4)
C
C     Find a shortest path between two given nodes
C
      INTEGER INODE(M),JNODE(M),ISPATH(N),IWORK2(N),IWORK3(M)
      REAL    WK4(N),ARCOST(M)
      LOGICAL IWORK1(N),IFIN
C
      DO 10 I = 1, N
         WK4(I) = BIG
         IWORK1(I) = .TRUE.
         IWORK2(I) = 0
 10   CONTINUE
      WK4(ISTART) = 0.
      I = ISTART
      IWORK1(ISTART) = .FALSE.
      NP = 0
      XLEN = 0
C
C     for each forward arc originating at node I calculate
C        the length of the path to node I
C
 20   IC = 0
      DO 30 K = 1, M
         IF (INODE(K) .EQ. I) THEN
            IC = IC + 1
            IWORK3(IC) = K
            ISPATH(IC) = JNODE(K)
         ENDIF
         IF (JNODE(K) .EQ. I) THEN
            IC = IC + 1
            IWORK3(IC) = K
            ISPATH(IC) = INODE(K)
         ENDIF
 30   CONTINUE
      IF (IC .GT. 0) THEN
         DO 40 L = 1, IC
            K = IWORK3(L)
            J = ISPATH(L)
            IF (IWORK1(J)) THEN
               D = WK4(I) + ARCOST(K)
               IF (D .LT. WK4(J)) THEN
                  WK4(J) = D
                  IWORK2(J) = K
               ENDIF
            ENDIF
 40      CONTINUE
      ENDIF
C
C     find the minimum potential
C
      D = BIG
      IENT = 0
      IFIN = .FALSE.
      DO 50 I = 1, N
         IF (IWORK1(I)) THEN
            IFIN = .TRUE.
            IF (WK4(I) .LT. D) THEN
               D = WK4(I)
               IENT = I
            ENDIF
         ENDIF
```

```
 50   CONTINUE
C
C     include the node in the current path
C
      IF (D .LT. BIG) THEN
         IWORK1(IENT) = .FALSE.
         IF (IENT .NE. LAST) THEN
            I = IENT
            GO TO 20
         ENDIF
      ELSE
         IF (IFIN) THEN
            NP = 1
            RETURN
         ENDIF
      ENDIF
      IJ = LAST
      NUMP = 1
      ISPATH(1) = LAST
 60   K = IWORK2(IJ)
         IF (INODE(K) .EQ. IJ)  THEN
            IJ = JNODE(K)
         ELSE
            IJ = INODE(K)
         ENDIF
         NUMP = NUMP + 1
         ISPATH(NUMP) = IJ
      IF (IJ .NE. ISTART) GO TO 60
      L = NUMP / 2
      J = NUMP
      DO 70 I = 1, L
         K = ISPATH(I)
         ISPATH(I) = ISPATH(J)
         ISPATH(J) = K
 70      J = J - 1
      XLEN = WK4(LAST)
C
      RETURN
      END
```

```
      SUBROUTINE MSPTRE (N,M,INODE,JNODE,ARCOST,BIG,ITREE,JTREE,XLEN,
     +                   IWORK1,IWORK2,IWORK3,IWORK4,IWORK5,WK6)
C
C     Finding a minimum spanning tree
C        the input graph is represented by a list of edges
C
C
      INTEGER INODE(M),JNODE(M),ITREE(N),JTREE(N),
     +        IWORK1(N),IWORK2(N),IWORK4(M),IWORK5(M)
      REAL    ARCOST(M),WK6(N)
      LOGICAL IWORK3(N)
C
      DO 10 I = 1, N
         WK6(I) = BIG
         IWORK3(I) = .TRUE.
         IWORK1(I) = 0
         IWORK2(I) = 0
         ITREE(I) = 0
         JTREE(I) = 0
   10 CONTINUE
C
C     find the first non-zero arc
C
      DO 20 IJ = 1, M
         IF (INODE(IJ) .NE. 0) THEN
            I = INODE(IJ)
            GO TO 30
         ENDIF
   20 CONTINUE
   30 WK6(I) = 0
      IWORK3(I) = .FALSE.
      XLEN = 0
      NNM1 = N - 1
      DO 90 JJ = 1, NNM1
         DO 40 K = 1, N
   40       WK6(K) = BIG
         DO 70 I = 1, N
C
C           for each forward arc originating at node I
C           calculate the length of the path to node I
C
            IF (.NOT. IWORK3(I)) THEN
               IC = 0
               DO 50 K = 1, M
                  IF (INODE(K) .EQ. I) THEN
                     IC = IC + 1
                     IWORK5(IC) = K
                     IWORK4(IC) = JNODE(K)
                  ENDIF
                  IF (JNODE(K) .EQ. I) THEN
                     IC = IC + 1
                     IWORK5(IC) = K
                     IWORK4(IC) = INODE(K)
                  ENDIF
   50          CONTINUE
               IF (IC .GT. 0) THEN
                  DO 60 L = 1, IC
                     K = IWORK5(L)
                     J = IWORK4(L)
                     IF (IWORK3(J)) THEN
                        D = XLEN + ARCOST(K)
                        IF (D .LT. WK6(J)) THEN
                           WK6(J) = D
```

```
                           IWORK1(J) = I
                           IWORK2(J) = K
                        ENDIF
                     ENDIF
 60               CONTINUE
               ENDIF
            ENDIF
 70      CONTINUE
C
C        find the minimum potential
C
         D = BIG
         IENT = 0
         DO 80 I = 1, N
            IF (IWORK3(I)) THEN
               IF (WK6(I) .LT. D) THEN
                  D = WK6(I)
                  IENT = I
                  ITR = IWORK1(I)
                  KK = IWORK2(I)
               ENDIF
            ENDIF
 80      CONTINUE
C
C        include the node in the current path
C
         IF (D .LT. BIG) THEN
            IWORK3(IENT) = .FALSE.
            XLEN = XLEN + ARCOST(KK)
            ITREE(JJ) = ITR
            JTREE(JJ) = IENT
         ENDIF
 90   CONTINUE
C
      RETURN
      END
```

Chapter 6

GRAPH PARTITIONING

A. Problem Description

Let V be the set of 2n nodes of a complete graph with an associated 2n by 2n symmetric cost matrix (c_{ij}) on its edges. The *graph partitioning problem* is to partition the nodes into two parts P and Q = V - P, each with n nodes, such that the total cost of the edges cut

$$\sum_{\substack{p \in P \\ q \in Q}} c_{pq}$$

is minimized.

The heuristic procedure to be described starts with any initial partition of the graph and then proceeds to decrease the total cost by a series of exchanges between the two sets until no further improvement can be achieved, whereby a partition with near minimum total cost is obtained. Note that this process can be repeated for as many random initial partitions as desire, and the best solution can be chosen among the local optimum solutions.

B. Algorithm

Step 1. Start with any initial partition P, Q of V.

Step 2. For each $p \in P$, $q \in Q$, define

$$F_p = \sum_{j \in Q} c_{pj} - \sum_{j \in P} c_{pj}$$

$$F_q = \sum_{i \in P} c_{iq} - \sum_{i \in Q} c_{iq} .$$

Choose nodes $s_1 \in P$, $t_1 \in Q$ such that

$$g_1 = F_{s_1} + F_{t_1} - 2c_{s_1 t_1}$$

is maximal. Note that s_1 and t_1 correspond to the largest possible cost gain from a single exchange. For $i = 2,\ldots,n$, choose sequentially

$$s_i \in P - \{s_1,\ldots,s_{i-1}\} \quad \text{and}$$

$$t_i \in Q - \{t_1,\ldots,t_{i-1}\}$$

such that

$$g_i = F_{s_i} + F_{t_i} - 2c_{s_i t_i}$$

is maximal; the F values are recalculated after each pair of s_i and t_i is chosen.

Step 3. If

$$\sum_{i=1}^{k} g_i \le 0 \quad \text{for all } k,$$

then stop (a local optimum solution is found); otherwise choose k such that

$$\sum_{j=1}^{k} g_i \quad \text{is maximal.}$$

Exchange the set $\{s_1,\ldots,s_k\}$ with the set $\{t_1,\ldots,t_k\}$, i.e., the sets P and Q are updated as follows :

$$P = P - \{s_1,\ldots,s_k\} + \{t_1,\ldots,t_k\}$$

$$Q = q - \{t_1,\ldots,t_k\} + \{s_1,\ldots,s_k\} .$$

Go to Step 2.

C. Subroutine PARTIT Parameters

Input :

N2 - total number of nodes in the complete graph, N2 is assumed to be even.

N - equal to N2 / 2.

COST - real symmetric matrix of dimension N2 by N2 containing the cost for each pair of nodes.

ICDIM - row dimension of matrix COST exactly as specified in the dimension statement of the calling program.

INIT - a boolean variable;
if INIT takes the value TRUE then as initial partition will be generated by PARTIT,
if INIT takes the value FALSE then an initial partition must be supplied.

IP, IQ - each is an integer vector of length N;
if INIT = TRUE then IP and IQ will be used only as working storages,
if INIT = FALSE then the initial two sets of the partition are stored in IP and IQ, respectively.

Output :

KP, KQ - each is an integer vector of length N, containing the two sets of the partition in the final solution.

TCOST - total cost in the final solution.

Working Storages :

WK1 - real vector of length N;
WK1(i) is the difference between external and internal cost of element i in the first partition.

WK2 - real vector of length N;
WK2(i) is the difference between external and internal cost of element i in the second partition.

WK3 - real vector of length N;
WK3(i) is the maximum gain of element i.

IWK4 - boolean vector of length N;
IWK4(i) indicates whether element i in the first partition has been investigated.

IWK5 - boolean vector of length N;
IWK5(i) indicates whether element i in the second partition has been investigated.

D. Test Example

Apply the graph partitioning heuristic algorithm to the complete graph of 10 nodes with the cost matrix given as follows :

```
0. 2. 4. 7. 4. 0. 0. 0. 5. 1.
2. 0. 3. 6. 3. 1. 1. 0. 1. 5.
4. 3. 0. 1. 2. 1. 0. 1. 0. 0.
7. 6. 1. 0. 0. 1. 0. 1. 0. 1.
4. 3. 2. 0. 0. 0. 1. 2. 0. 4.
0. 1. 1. 1. 0. 0. 0. 1. 0. 1.
0. 1. 0. 0. 1. 0. 0. 0. 1. 3.
0. 0. 1. 1. 2. 1. 0. 0. 1. 1.
5. 1. 0. 0. 0. 0. 1. 1. 0. 1.
1. 5. 0. 1. 4. 1. 3. 1. 1. 0.
```

Main Program

```
      INTEGER IP(5),IQ(5),KP(5),KQ(5)
      REAL    COST(10,10),WK1(5),WK2(5),WK3(5)
      LOGICAL IWK4(5),IWK5(5),INIT
C
      READ(*,10) N2
   10 FORMAT(I3)
      DO 20 I = 1, N2
   20    READ(*,30) (COST(I,J),J=1,N2)
   30    FORMAT(10F3.0)
      N = N2 / 2
      ICDIM = 10
      INIT = .TRUE.
      CALL PARTIT(N2,N,COST,ICDIM,INIT,IP,IQ,KP,KQ,TCOST,
     +            WK1,WK2,WK3,IWK4,IWK5)
      WRITE(*,40) (KP(I),I=1,N)
   40 FORMAT(/'  FIRST SET  : ',5I3)
      WRITE(*,50) (KQ(I),I=1,N)
   50 FORMAT(/'  SECOND SET : ',5I3)
      WRITE(*,60) TCOST
   60 FORMAT(/'  TOTAL COST  =',F10.1)
      STOP
      END
```

Input Data

```
 10
 0. 2. 4. 7. 4. 0. 0. 0. 5. 1.
 2. 0. 3. 6. 3. 1. 1. 0. 1. 5.
 4. 3. 0. 1. 2. 1. 0. 1. 0. 0.
 7. 6. 1. 0. 0. 1. 0. 1. 0. 1.
 4. 3. 2. 0. 0. 0. 1. 2. 0. 4.
 0. 1. 1. 1. 0. 0. 0. 1. 0. 1.
 0. 1. 0. 0. 1. 0. 0. 0. 1. 3.
 0. 0. 1. 1. 2. 1. 0. 0. 1. 1.
 5. 1. 0. 0. 0. 0. 1. 1. 0. 1.
 1. 5. 0. 1. 4. 1. 3. 1. 1. 0.
```

Output Results

```
  FIRST SET  :   9  3  1  4  2

  SECOND SET :   5 10  7  6  8

  TOTAL COST  =       25.0
```

```
      SUBROUTINE PARTIT (N2,N,COST,ICDIM,INIT,IP,IQ,KP,KQ,TCOST,
     +                    WK1,WK2,WK3,IWK4,IWK5)
C
C     Graph partitioning heuristic
C
      INTEGER IP(N),IQ(N),KP(N),KQ(N)
      REAL    COST(ICDIM,1),WK1(N),WK2(N),WK3(N)
      LOGICAL IWK4(N),IWK5(N),INIT
C
C     initial partitioning
C
      IF (INIT)  THEN
         DO 10 I = 1, N
            IP(I) = I
            IQ(I) = I + N
 10      CONTINUE
      ENDIF
C
C     set the flags
C
 20   DO 30 I = 1, N
         IWK4(I) = .TRUE.
         IWK5(I) = .TRUE.
 30   CONTINUE
      TCOST = 0.
      DO 40 I = 1, N
         DO 40 J = 1, N
 40         TCOST = TCOST + COST(IP(I),IQ(J))
      SMALL = - 2.0 * TCOST
C
C        calculate the external cost of each element in the first
C        partition
C
      DO 70 I = 1, N
         TOT1 = 0.
         DO 50 J = 1, N
 50         TOT1 = TOT1 + COST(IP(I),IQ(J))
C
C        calculate the internal cost of each element in the first
C        partition
C
         TOT2 = 0.
         DO 60 K = 1, N
 60         TOT2 = TOT2 + COST(IP(I),IP(K))
C
C        calculate the difference between external and internal
C        cost
C
         WK1(I) = TOT1 - TOT2
 70   CONTINUE
      DO 100 I = 1, N
C
C        calculate the external cost of each element in the second
C        partition
C
         TOT1 = 0.
         DO 80 J = 1, N
 80         TOT1 = TOT1 + COST(IQ(I),IP(J))
C
C        calculate the internal cost of each element in the second
C        partition
C
         TOT2 = 0.
```

```
        DO 90 K = 1, N
 90        TOT2 = TOT2 + COST(IQ(I),IQ(K))
C
C       calculate the difference between external and internal
C       cost
C
        WK2(I) = TOT1 - TOT2
 100  CONTINUE
      DO 140 I = 1, N
C
C       choose IA from the first partition and IB from the second
C       partition such that the gain is maximum
C
        TMAX = SMALL
        DO 120 J = 1, N
           IF (IWK4(J))  THEN
              DO 110 K = 1, N
                 IF (IWK5(K))  THEN
                    GAIN = WK1(J) + WK2(K) - 2.0*COST(IP(J),IQ(K))
                    IF (GAIN .GT. TMAX)  THEN
                       TMAX = GAIN
                       IA = IP(J)
                       IB = IQ(K)
                       IND1 = J
                       IND2 = K
                    ENDIF
                 ENDIF
 110          CONTINUE
           ENDIF
 120    CONTINUE
C
        WK3(I) = TMAX
        KP(I) = IA
        KQ(I) = IB
        IWK4(IND1) = .FALSE.
        IWK5(IND2) = .FALSE.
C
C       recalculate the cost differences
C
        DO 130 J = 1, N
           IF (IWK4(J))
     +        WK1(J) = WK1(J)+2.0*COST(IP(J),IA)-2.0*COST(IP(J),IB)
           IF (IWK5(J))
     +        WK2(J) = WK2(J)+2.0*COST(IQ(J),IB)-2.0*COST(IQ(J),IA)
 130    CONTINUE
 140  CONTINUE
C
C     choose K such that WK3(K) is maximal
C
      TMAX = SMALL
      DO 160 I = 1, N
         TOT1 = 0.
         DO 150 J = 1, I
 150        TOT1 = TOT1 + WK3(J)
         IF (TOT1 .GT. TMAX)  THEN
            TMAX = TOT1
            K = I
         ENDIF
 160  CONTINUE
C
C     exchange the two elements found above,
C     iterate until no reduction in cost can be obtained
C
```

```
      IF (TMAX .GT. 0)  THEN
         DO 170 I = 1, K
            IP(I) = KQ(I)
            IQ(I) = KP(I)
 170     CONTINUE
         K1 = K + 1
         DO 180 I = K1, N
            IP(I) = KP(I)
            IQ(I) = KQ(I)
 180     CONTINUE
         GO TO 20
      ENDIF
C
      RETURN
      END
```

Chapter 7

K-MEDIAN LOCATION

A. Problem Description

Let $C = (c_{ij})$ be an m by n matrix, and k be an integer $1 \le k < m$. The *k-median location problem* is to find a subset S of k rows of C that maximizes

$$\sum_{j=1}^{n} \max_{i \in S} c_{ij} .$$

The heuristic procedure to be described finds a near-optimum solution in time proportional to mn.

B. Algorithm

Step 1. Start with a random set of k rows of C. Without loss of generality, the initial rows are assumed to be the first k rows of C.

Step 2. Augment the k initial rows by one row chosen from the $m - k$ unused rows, to make a set of $k + 1$ rows. Compute which of these $k + 1$ rows contributes the least to the cost of the set and remove it. Move to the next row in the unused ones and add it to the current k rows. The process terminates when all the $m - k$ currently unused rows have been examined without finding a profitable replacement.

Remarks

Note that the local optimum solution found by the algorithm has the property that no replacement of any row in the solution by any other unused row can improve its cost. Obviously, the algorithm can be used to find more local optimum solutions from different initial solutions.

C. Subroutine KMED Parameters

Input :

- M - number of rows of the cost matrix.
- N - number of columns of the cost matrix.
- C - real matrix of dimension M by N containing the cost.
- K - the number of maximizing rows.
- ICDIM - row dimension of matrix C exactly as specified in the dimension statement of the calling program.

Output :

- ISOL - integer vector of length M; the row numbers of the maximizing set are contained in the first K elements of ISOL.

Working Storages :

- WORK1 - real vector of length N; WORK1(i) is the first largest element of column i among the candidate set of rows.
- WORK2 - real vector of length N; WORK2(i) is the second largest element of column i among the candidate set of rows.
- WORK3 - real vector of length M; WORK3(i) is the decrease in value if row i is removed from the candidate set of rows.
- WORK4 - real vector of length M; WORK4(i) is the change in WORK3(i) if row i is removed from the candidate set plus an extra row.
- IWK5 - integer vector of length N; IWK5(i) is the row number corresponding to WORK1(i).
- IWK6 - integer vector of length N; IWK6(i) is the row number corresponding to WORK2(i).

D. Test Example

With $M = 10$ and $N = 15$, the cost matrix (c_{ij}) is given as follows :

2.	3.	0.	6.	5.	2.	3.	2.	4.	9.	2.	0.	8.	7.	3.
4.	8.	6.	0.	8.	1.	3.	3.	4.	1.	1.	9.	3.	8.	3.
0.	8.	4.	6.	2.	3.	2.	6.	6.	6.	5.	7.	9.	9.	0.
9.	7.	2.	6.	4.	2.	1.	5.	9.	0.	7.	1.	1.	4.	2.
7.	4.	5.	3.	3.	4.	5.	0.	3.	4.	3.	3.	8.	4.	9.
6.	1.	1.	7.	7.	9.	7.	4.	6.	7.	2.	2.	1.	5.	0.
7.	4.	0.	7.	7.	4.	3.	2.	4.	3.	9.	5.	1.	8.	5.
5.	1.	5.	7.	0.	8.	4.	6.	5.	6.	4.	3.	5.	2.	1.
1.	2.	5.	2.	4.	7.	4.	7.	0.	9.	7.	5.	2.	1.	7.
7.	9.	0.	0.	6.	3.	0.	8.	3.	9.	1.	7.	1.	6.	5.

Find a subset S of 4 rows of the matrix that maximizes

$$\sum_{j=1}^{15} \max_{i \in S} c_{ij} .$$

Main Program

```
      REAL C(10,15),WORK1(15),WORK2(15),WORK3(10),WORK4(10)
      INTEGER ISOL(10),IWK5(15),IWK6(15)
C
      READ(*,10) M,N,K
 10   FORMAT(3I3)
      DO 20 I = 1, M
 20      READ(*,30) (C(I,J),J=1,N)
 30      FORMAT(15F3.0)
      ICDIM = 10
C
      CALL KMED(M,N,C,K,ICDIM,ISOL,
     +          WORK1,WORK2,WORK3,WORK4,IWK5,IWK6)
C
      WRITE(*,40) (ISOL(I),I=1,K)
 40   FORMAT(/'  THE K ROWS FOUND :  ',4I4)
C
      STOP
      END
```

Input Data

```
 10 15  4
 2. 3. 0. 6. 5. 2. 3. 2. 4. 9. 2. 0. 8. 7. 3.
 4. 8. 6. 0. 8. 1. 3. 3. 4. 1. 1. 9. 3. 8. 3.
 0. 8. 4. 6. 2. 3. 2. 6. 6. 6. 5. 7. 9. 9. 0.
 9. 7. 2. 6. 4. 2. 1. 5. 9. 0. 7. 1. 1. 4. 2.
 7. 4. 5. 3. 3. 4. 5. 0. 3. 4. 3. 3. 8. 4. 9.
 6. 1. 1. 7. 7. 9. 7. 4. 6. 7. 2. 2. 1. 5. 0.
 7. 4. 0. 7. 7. 4. 3. 2. 4. 3. 9. 5. 1. 8. 5.
 5. 1. 5. 7. 0. 8. 4. 6. 5. 6. 4. 3. 5. 2. 1.
 1. 2. 5. 2. 4. 7. 4. 7. 0. 9. 7. 5. 2. 1. 7.
 7. 9. 0. 0. 6. 3. 0. 8. 3. 9. 1. 7. 1. 6. 5.
```

Output Results

```
  THE K ROWS FOUND :     5   2   6   4
```

```
      SUBROUTINE KMED (M,N,C,K,ICDIM,ISOL,
     +                 WORK1,WORK2,WORK3,WORK4,IWK5,IWK6)
C
C     K-median heuristic
C
      REAL    C(ICDIM,N),WORK1(N),WORK2(N),WORK3(M),WORK4(M)
      INTEGER IWK5(N),IWK6(N),ISOL(M)
C
C     compute the machine epsilon
C
      EPS = 1.0
 10   EPS = EPS / 2.0
         TOL   = 1.0 + EPS
         IF (TOL .GT. 1.0)  GO TO 10
      EPS = SQRT(EPS)
C
C     compute the machine infinity
C
      BIG = 1.0E6
 20   BIG = BIG * BIG
         TOL = 1.0 + BIG
         IF (TOL .GT. BIG)  GO TO 20
      BIG = BIG * BIG
C
      DO 30 I = 1, M
 30      WORK3(I) = 0.
      IF (K .EQ. 1)  THEN
C
C        obtain the optimal solution when K = 1
C
         OPTVAL = -BIG
         DO 50 I = 1, M
            SUM = 0.
            DO 40 J = 1, N
 40            SUM = SUM + C(I,J)
            IF (SUM .GT. OPTVAL)  THEN
               OPTVAL = SUM
               INDEX = I
            ENDIF
 50      CONTINUE
         ISOL(1) = INDEX
         RETURN
      ENDIF
C
C     find the largest and second-largest elements among the first
C     M elements of column J;  store them in WORK1(J) and WORK2(J)
C
      DO 80 I = 1, N
         WORK1(I) = -BIG
         DO 60 J = 1, K
            IF (C(J,I) .GT. WORK1(I))  THEN
               WORK1(I) = C(J,I)
               IWK5(I) = J
            ENDIF
 60      CONTINUE
         WORK2(I) = -BIG
         DO 70 J = 1, K
            IF (C(J,I) .GT. WORK2(I) .AND. J .NE. IWK5(I))  THEN
               WORK2(I) = C(J,I)
               IWK6(I) = J
            ENDIF
 70      CONTINUE
 80   CONTINUE
```

```
      DO 100 I = 1, K
         TOT1 = 0.
         DO 90 J = 1, N
            IF (IWK5(J) .EQ. I)  TOT1 = TOT1 + WORK1(J) - WORK2(J)
 90      CONTINUE
         WORK3(I) = TOT1
 100  CONTINUE
C
      DO 110 I = 1, M
 110     ISOL(I) = I
C
      IFLAG = 0
      IR = K
      MMK = M - K
C
 120  IF ((IR+1) .GT. M)  IR = K
      IR = IR + 1
C
      DO 130 I = 1, K
 130     WORK4(ISOL(I)) = 0.
      WORK4(ISOL(IR)) = 0.
C
C     find out which of the K+1 rows will make the objective
C         value decrease the least if the row is removed
C
      DO 140 J = 1, N
         Z = C(ISOL(IR),J)
         IF (Z .GT. WORK2(J) .AND. Z .LE. WORK1(J))  THEN
            WORK4(IWK5(J)) = WORK4(IWK5(J)) - Z + WORK2(J)
         ELSE
            IF (Z .GT. WORK1(J))  THEN
               WORK4(ISOL(IR)) = WORK4(ISOL(IR)) + Z - WORK1(J)
               WORK4(IWK5(J)) = WORK4(IWK5(J)) - WORK1(J) + WORK2(J)
            ENDIF
         ENDIF
 140  CONTINUE
C
C     determine which row to remove
C
      TMIN = BIG
      DO 150 IJ = 1, K
         I = ISOL(IJ)
         TEMP = WORK3(I) + WORK4(I)
         IF (TEMP .LT. TMIN)  THEN
            TMIN = TEMP
            L = IJ
         ENDIF
 150  CONTINUE
C
      I = ISOL(IR)
      TEMP = WORK3(I) + WORK4(I)
      IF ((TEMP .LE. TMIN) .OR. (ABS(TEMP - TMIN) .LE. EPS)) THEN
         IFLAG = IFLAG + 1
         IF (IFLAG .EQ. MMK)  RETURN
         GO TO 120
      ENDIF
C
      IFLAG = 0
      TOT1 = 0.
      DO 160 I = 1, N
         IF (C(ISOL(IR),I) .GT. WORK1(I))
     +            TOT1 = TOT1 + C(ISOL(IR),I) - WORK1(I)
 160  CONTINUE
```

```
      WORK3(ISOL(IR)) = TOT1
C
C     update all arrays after exchanging two rows
C
      DO 190 J = 1, N
         Z = C(ISOL(IR),J)
         IF (Z .LE. WORK2(J))  THEN
            IF (ISOL(L) .EQ. IWK5(J))  THEN
C
C              replacing the largest element by something no better
C              than the third largest
C
               WORK1(J) = WORK2(J)
               IWK5(J) = IWK6(J)
               W = -BIG
               DO 170 IJ = 1, K
                  II = ISOL(IJ)
                  IF (C(II,J) .GT. W .AND. II .NE. IWK5(J))  THEN
                     W = C(II,J)
                     IW = II
                  ENDIF
  170          CONTINUE
               II = ISOL(IR)
               IF (C(II,J) .GT. W .AND. II .NE. IWK5(J))  THEN
                  W = C(II,J)
                  IW = II
               ENDIF
               WORK3(IWK6(J)) = WORK3(IWK6(J)) - W + WORK2(J)
               WORK2(J) = W
               IWK6(J) = IW
            ENDIF
            IF (ISOL(L) .EQ. IWK6(J))  THEN
C
C              replacing the second largest element by something no
C              better than the third largest
C
               W = -BIG
               DO 180 IJ = 1, K
                  II = ISOL(IJ)
                  IF (C(II,J) .GT. W .AND. II .NE. IWK5(J)
     +                              .AND. II .NE. IWK6(J))  THEN
                     W = C(II,J)
                     IW = II
                  ENDIF
  180          CONTINUE
               II = ISOL(IR)
               IF (C(II,J) .GT. W  .AND.  II .NE. IWK5(J)
     +                             .AND.  II .NE. IWK6(J))  THEN
                  W = C(II,J)
                  IW = II
               ENDIF
               WORK3(IWK5(J)) = WORK3(IWK5(J)) - W + WORK2(J)
               WORK2(J) = W
               IWK6(J) = IW
            ENDIF
         ELSE
            IF (Z .GT. WORK2(J) .AND. Z .LE. WORK1(J))  THEN
               IF (ISOL(L) .EQ. IWK5(J))  THEN
C
C                 replacing the largest element by a new and smaller
C                 largest element
C
                  WORK1(J) = Z
```

```
                  IWK5(J) = ISOL(IR)
                  WORK4(ISOL(IR)) = WORK4(ISOL(IR)) + Z - WORK2(J)
               ELSE
C
C                 Z becomes the new second largest element
C
                  WORK3(IWK5(J)) = WORK3(IWK5(J)) - Z + WORK2(J)
                  WORK2(J) = Z
                  IWK6(J) = ISOL(IR)
               ENDIF
            ELSE
               IF (Z .GT. WORK1(J))  THEN
                  IF (ISOL(L) .EQ. IWK5(J))  THEN
C
C                    replacing the largest element by a new largest
C                    element
C
                     WORK4(ISOL(IR)) = WORK4(ISOL(IR)) +
     +                                 WORK1(J) - WORK2(J)
                     IWK5(J) = ISOL(IR)
                     WORK1(J) = Z
                  ELSE
C
C                    Z becomes the largest element
C
                     WORK3(IWK5(J)) = WORK3(IWK5(J)) -
     +                                WORK1(J) + WORK2(J)
                     WORK2(J) = WORK1(J)
                     WORK1(J) = Z
                     IWK6(J) = IWK5(J)
                     IWK5(J) = ISOL(IR)
                  ENDIF
               ENDIF
            ENDIF
         ENDIF
  190 CONTINUE
C
C     iterate until no improvement by exchange can be found
C
      ITMP = ISOL(L)
      ISOL(L) = ISOL(IR)
      ISOL(IR) = ITMP
      WORK3(ISOL(L)) = WORK4(ISOL(L))
      K1 = K + 1
      DO 200 I = K1, M
  200    WORK3(ISOL(I)) = 0.
      GO TO 120
C
      END
```

Chapter 8

K-CENTER LOCATION

A. Problem Description

Let V be the set of nodes of a complete undirected graph of n nodes with edge weights $c_{ij} \geq 0$ associated with edge (i,j) for all nodes i, j in V; and $c_{ii} = 0$. Given an integer k, $1 \leq k \leq n$, the *k-center location problem* is to find a subset S of V of size at most k such that

$$Z = \max_{i \in V} \min_{j \in S} c_{ij}$$

is minimized.

In general, it is very hard to develop efficient algorithms that yield good approximate solutions to the problem. However, in the particular case when the triangle inequality is satisfied, i.e.,

$$c_{ij} + c_{jk} \geq c_{ik} \qquad \text{for all} \quad 1 \leq i,j,k \leq n,$$

then solutions close to the optimum can be found in a relatively short computer time. In fact, the approximate solution value Z computed by the algorithm to be described next is guaranteed to be at most two times the value of an optimal solution.

B. Algorithm

Step 1. Let m be the total number of edges in the complete graph. Sort the edges in a sequence

$$(e_1, e_2, \ldots, e_m)$$

of nondecreasing edge weights.

If $k = n$ then set

$$S = V$$

and stop; otherwise set

$$LOW = 1 \quad \text{and} \quad HIGH = m.$$

Step 2. Set

$$MID = \lfloor (HIGH + LOW) / 2 \rfloor,$$
$$P = \text{empty set},$$
$$Q = V.$$

Let H be the graph consisting of edges

$$e_1, e_2, \ldots, e_{MID}.$$

For every node x in Q,
include x in the set P, and
delete node x and all nodes adjacent to x in H from the set Q.

Step 3. If the size of the set P is not greater than k, then set

$$HIGH = MID \quad \text{and}$$
$$S = P;$$

otherwise set

$$LOW = MID.$$

Step 4. If

$$HIGH = LOW + 1$$

then output the set S and stop;
otherwise return to Step 2 to continue the binary search.

C. Subroutine KCENTR Parameters

Input :

N - number of nodes in the complete graph.

M - equal to N(N-1)/2.

COST - real symmetric matrix of dimension N by N containing the cost for each pair of nodes.

KMAX - the maximum size of the subset of nodes to be found.

ICDIM - row dimension of matrix COST exactly as specified in the dimension statement of the calling program.

Output :

KNUM - the size of the subset of nodes found, KNUM ≤ KMAX.

KSET - the nodes of the solution are stored in KSET(i), i=1,2,...,KNUM.

Working Storages :

IWK1 - integer matrix of dimension N by N; stores the edge number of the graph in the order of increasing edge weight.

IWK2 - boolean vector of length N; IWK2(i) indicates whether node i has been selected.

IWK3 - integer vector of length N; stores the current solution set.

IWK4 - integer vector of length M; IWK4(i) is the pointer to the original arc i after the edges are sorted.

IWK5 - integer vector of length M; pointer array for keeping the order of the original edges.

WORK6 - real vector of length M; stores the upper triangular COST matrix of the original graph in the order of rows.

D. Test Example

The edge weights c_{ij} of a complete graph G with 10 nodes is given as follows :

0.	15.	72.	51.	50.	59.	53.	68.	11.	33.
15.	0.	66.	44.	43.	45.	56.	65.	9.	35.
72.	66.	0.	104.	23.	77.	38.	11.	62.	44.
51.	44.	104.	0.	82.	41.	99.	106.	52.	79.
50.	43.	23.	82.	0.	59.	26.	25.	39.	28.
59.	45.	77.	41.	59.	0.	82.	83.	52.	70.
53.	56.	38.	99.	26.	82.	0.	28.	47.	21.
68.	65.	11.	106.	25.	83.	28.	0.	59.	37.
11.	9.	62.	52.	39.	52.	47.	59.	0.	27.
33.	35.	44.	79.	28.	70.	21.	37.	27.	0.

Find a subset S of nodes (or centers) of size at most 4 such that

$$\max_{i \in G} \min_{j \in S} c_{ij}$$

is minimized.

Main Program

```
      INTEGER KSET(10),IWK1(10,10),IWK2(10),
     +        IWK3(10),IWK4(45),IWK5(45)
      REAL    COST(10,10),WORK6(45)
C
      READ(*,10) N,KMAX
 10   FORMAT(2I4)
      DO 20 I = 1, N
 20      READ(*,30)  (COST(I,J),J=1,N)
 30      FORMAT(10F6.1)
C
      M = (N * (N - 1)) / 2
      ICDIM = 10
      CALL KCENTR(N,M,COST,KMAX,ICDIM,KNUM,KSET,
     +            IWK1,IWK2,IWK3,IWK4,IWK5,WORK6)
      WRITE(*,40) (KSET(I),I=1,KNUM)
 40   FORMAT(/'  THE CENTERS FOUND :    ',4I4)
C
      STOP
      END
```

Input Data

```
  10   4
   0.0  15.0  72.0  51.0  50.0  59.0  53.0  68.0  11.0  33.0
  15.0   0.0  66.0  44.0  43.0  45.0  56.0  65.0   9.0  35.0
  72.0  66.0   0.0 104.0  23.0  77.0  38.0  11.0  62.0  44.0
  51.0  44.0 104.0   0.0  82.0  41.0  99.0 106.0  52.0  79.0
  50.0  43.0  23.0  82.0   0.0  59.0  26.0  25.0  39.0  28.0
  59.0  45.0  77.0  41.0  59.0   0.0  82.0  83.0  52.0  70.0
  53.0  56.0  38.0  99.0  26.0  82.0   0.0  28.0  47.0  21.0
  68.0  65.0  11.0 106.0  25.0  83.0  28.0   0.0  59.0  37.0
  11.0   9.0  62.0  52.0  39.0  52.0  47.0  59.0   0.0  27.0
  33.0  35.0  44.0  79.0  28.0  70.0  21.0  37.0  27.0   0.0
```

Output Results

```
 THE CENTERS FOUND :       9   5   4   6
```

```
      SUBROUTINE KCENTR (N,M,COST,KMAX,ICDIM,KNUM,KSET,
     +                   IWK1,IWK2,IWK3,IWK4,IWK5,WORK6)
C
C     K-center heuristic
C
      INTEGER KSET(N),IWK1(N,N),IWK2(N),IWK3(N),IWK4(M),IWK5(M)
      REAL    COST(ICDIM,1),WORK6(M)
C
      N1 = N - 1
      GREAT = 1.0
      DO 20 I = 1, N1
         I1 = I + 1
         DO 10 J = I1, N
 10         GREAT = GREAT + COST(I,J)
 20   CONTINUE
C
C     special case when KMAX = 1
C
      SMALL = GREAT
      DO 40 I = 1, N
         BIG = -GREAT
         DO 30 J = 1, N
            IF (J .NE. I)  THEN
               IF (COST(I,J) .GT. BIG)  THEN
                  BIG = COST(I,J)
                  NUMK = I
               ENDIF
            ENDIF
 30      CONTINUE
         IF (BIG .LT. SMALL)  THEN
            SMALL = BIG
            KNUM =  NUMK
         ENDIF
 40   CONTINUE
C
      IFIRST = KNUM
C
C     return the optimal solution if KMAX = 1
C
      IF (KMAX .EQ. 1)  THEN
         KNUM = 1
         KSET(1) = IFIRST
         RETURN
      ENDIF
C
C     sort the edges in order of increasing cost
C
      K = 0
      DO 60 I = 1, N1
         I1 = I + 1
         DO 50 J = I1, N
            K = K + 1
 50         WORK6(K) = COST(I,J)
 60   CONTINUE
C
      CALL SORTI(M,WORK6,IWK4)
      DO 70 I = 1, M
         J = IWK4(I)
 70      IWK5(J) = I
      K = 0
      DO 90 I = 1, N1
         I1 = I + 1
         DO 80 J = I1, N
```

```
            K = K + 1
            IWK1(I,J) = IWK5(K)
 80         IWK1(J,I) = IWK5(K)
 90   CONTINUE
C
C     binary search
C
      LOW = 1
      IHIGH = M
C
 100  IF (IHIGH .NE. (LOW + 1))  THEN
         MID = (IHIGH + LOW) / 2
C
C        restrict to the subgraph with the original N nodes
C          but only having the first MID number of edges
C
         NUMK = 0
         NCHECK = N
         DO 110 I = 1, N
 110        IWK2(I) = 0
C
         INODE = IFIRST
 120     NUMK = NUMK + 1
C
C        include node INODE into the solution set
C
         IWK3(NUMK) = INODE
C
C        consider all nodes adjacent to node INODE
C
         DO 140 K = 1, N
            IF (K .NE. INODE)  THEN
               IF (IWK1(K,INODE) .LE. MID)  THEN
C
C                 node K is adjacent to node INODE;
C                   delete node K from the subgraph
C
                  IF (IWK2(K) .EQ. 0)  THEN
                     NCHECK = NCHECK - 1
                     IWK2(K) = 2
                  ENDIF
C
C                 delete all nodes adjacent to node K
C                   from the subgraph
C
                  DO 130 L = 1, N
                     IF (IWK2(L) .EQ. 0) THEN
                        IF (L .NE. K)  THEN
                           IF (IWK1(K,L) .LE. MID)  THEN
C
C                             node L is adjacent to node K;
C                             delete node L from the subgraph
C
                              NCHECK = NCHECK - 1
                              IWK2(L) = 2
                           ENDIF
                        ENDIF
                     ENDIF
 130              CONTINUE
               ENDIF
            ENDIF
 140     CONTINUE
C
```

```
C        mark node INODE as being already selected
C
         IF (IWK2(INODE) .EQ. 0)  THEN
            NCHECK = NCHECK - 1
         ENDIF
         IWK2(INODE) = 1
C
C        continue the binary search if the subgraph is nonempty
C
         IF (NCHECK .GT. 0)  THEN
C
C           pick the next center by the greedy heuristic
C
            IF (NCHECK .LE. 2)  THEN
               DO 150 I = 1, N
                  IF (IWK2(I) .EQ. 0)  THEN
                     INODE = I
                     GOTO 120
                  ENDIF
 150           CONTINUE
            ENDIF
            SMALL = GREAT
            DO 170 I = 1, N
               IF (IWK2(I) .EQ. 0)  THEN
                  BIG = -GREAT
                  DO 160 J = 1, N
                     IF (IWK2(J) .EQ. 0)  THEN
                        IF (J .NE. I)  THEN
                           IF (COST(I,J) .GT. BIG)  THEN
                              BIG = COST(I,J)
                              NUM1 = I
                           ENDIF
                        ENDIF
                     ENDIF
 160              CONTINUE
                  IF (BIG .LT. SMALL)  THEN
                     SMALL = BIG
                     NUM2 =  NUM1
                  ENDIF
               ENDIF
 170        CONTINUE
C
            INODE = NUM2
            GOTO 120
         ENDIF
C
         IF (NUMK .LE. KMAX)  THEN
C
C           store up the temporary solution set
C
            IHIGH = MID
            KNUM = NUMK
            DO 180 I = 1, KNUM
 180           KSET(I) = IWK3(I)
         ELSE
            LOW = MID
         ENDIF
C
         GOTO 100
      ENDIF
C
      RETURN
      END
```

```
      SUBROUTINE SORTI (N,A,IPOINT)
C
C     Heapsort :  nondecreasing order sorting
C
      INTEGER  IPOINT(N)
      REAL     A(N)
C
      DO 10 I = 1, N
 10      IPOINT(I) = I
      J1 = N
      J2 = N / 2
      J3 = J2
      ATEMP = A(J2)
      JPONT = IPOINT(J2)
C
 20   J4 = J2 + J2
      IF (J4 .LE. J1)  THEN
         IF (J4 .LT. J1)  THEN
            IF (A(J4+1) .GE. A(J4))  J4 = J4 + 1
         ENDIF
         IF (ATEMP .LT. A(J4))  THEN
            A(J2) = A(J4)
            IPOINT(J2) = IPOINT(J4)
            J2 = J4
            GOTO 20
         ENDIF
      ENDIF
C
      A(J2) = ATEMP
      IPOINT(J2) = JPONT
      IF (J3 .GT. 1)  THEN
         J3 = J3 - 1
         ATEMP = A(J3)
         JPONT = IPOINT(J3)
         J2 = J3
         GOTO 20
      ENDIF
C
      IF (J1 .GE. 2)  THEN
         ATEMP = A(J1)
         JPONT = IPOINT(J1)
         A(J1) = A(1)
         IPOINT(J1) = IPOINT(1)
         J1 = J1 - 1
         J2 = J3
         GOTO 20
      ENDIF
C
      RETURN
      END
```

LIST OF SUBROUTINES

BIBLIOGRAPHIC NOTES

Chapter 1. [Integer Linear Programming]

The linear search heuristic approach for solving the general integer linear programming problem has been suggested by F. S. Hillier, "Efficient heuristic procedure for integer linear programming with an interior", *Operations Research* 17(1969), 600-637.

Chapter 2. [Zero-one Linear Programming]

The effective gradient method for solving the multi-dimensional knapsack type zero-one programming problem has been developed by Y. Toyoda, "A simplified algorithm for obtaining approximate solutions to zero-one programming problems", *Management Science* 21(1975), 1417-1427.

Chapter 3. [Zero-one Knapsack Problem]

The fully polynomial-time approximation scheme for solving the zero-one knapsack problem has been constructed by O. H. Ibarra and C. E. Kim, "Fast approximation algorithms for the knapsack and sum of subset problems", *Journal of the Association for Computing Machinery* 22(1975), 463-468.

The sorting subroutine uses the heapsort method which originated with J.W.J. Williams, "Algorithm 232 : Heapsort", *Communications of the ACM* 7(1964), 347-348, and was improved by R. W. Floyd, "Algorithm 245 : Treesort 3", *Communications of the ACM* 7(1964), 701.

Chapter 4. [Traveling Salesman Problem]

The approximate algorithm for the triangle inequality traveling salesman problem was discovered by N. Christofides, "Worst-case analysis of a new heuristic for the traveling salesman problem", Management Science Research Report No. 388, Carnegie-Mellon University, 1976.

The Euler circuit algorithm is due to Fleury, see E. Lucas, *Récreations Mathématiques* IV, Paris, 1921.

The minimum spanning tree algorithm follows from R. C. Prim, "Shortest connection networks and some generalizations", *Bell System Technical Journal* 36(1957), 1389-1401.

The subroutine for finding a minimum weight perfect matching in a graph is modified from the code of R. E. Burkard and U. Derigs, *Assignment and Matching Problems: Soultion methods with FORTRAN-Programs*, Lecture Notes in Economics and Mathematical Systems, Vol. 184, Springer-Verlag, 1980.

Chapter 5. [Steiner Tree Problem]

The Steiner tree heuristic algorithm comes from L. Kou, G. Markowsky and L. Berman, "A fast algorithm for Steiner trees", Research Report RC 7390, IBM Thomas J. Watson Research Center, Yorktown Heights, New York, 1978.

The shortest path algorithm originates from E. W. Dijkstra, "A note on two problems in connexion with graphs", *Numerische Mathematik* 1(1959), 269-271.

The minimum spanning tree algorithm follows from R. C. Prim, "Shortest connection networks and some generalizations", *Bell System Technical Journal* 36(1957), 1389-1401.

Chapter 6. [Graph Partitioning]

The two-way graph partitioning heuristic algorithm comes from B. W. Kernighan and S. Lin, "An efficient heuristic procedure for partitioning graphs", *Bell System Technical Journal* 49(1970), 291-307.

Chapter 7. [K-median Location]

The k-median location heuristic algorithm is from B. W. Kernighan and S. Lin, "Heuristic solution of a signal design optimization problem", *Bell System Technical Journal* 52(1973), 1145-1159.

Chapter 8. [K-center Location]

The two-approximation algorithm for the k-center problem with triangle inequality is credited to D. S. Hochbaum and D. B. Shmoys, "A best possible heuristic for the k-center problem", *Mathematics of Operations Research* 10(1985), 180-184.

The sorting subroutine uses the heapsort method which originated with J.W.J. Williams, "Algorithm 232 : Heapsort", *Communications of the ACM* 7(1964), 347-348, and was improved by R. W. Floyd, "Algorithm 245 : Treesort 3", *Communications of the ACM* 7(1964), 701.

Vol. 184: R. E. Burkard and U. Derigs, Assignment and Matching Problems: Solution Methods with FORTRAN-Programs. VIII, 148 pages. 1980.

Vol. 185: C. C. von Weizsäcker, Barriers to Entry. VI, 220 pages. 1980.

Vol. 186: Ch.-L. Hwang and K. Yoon, Multiple Attribute Decision Making – Methods and Applications. A State-of-the-Art-Survey. XI, 259 pages. 1981.

Vol. 187: W. Hock, K. Schittkowski, Test Examples for Nonlinear Programming Codes. V. 178 pages. 1981.

Vol. 188: D. Bös, Economic Theory of Public Enterprise. VII, 142 pages. 1981.

Vol. 189: A.-P. Lüthi, Messung wirtschaftlicher Ungleichheit. IX, 287 pages. 1981.

Vol. 190: J. N. Morse, Organizations: Multiple Agents with Multiple Criteria. Proceedings, 1980. VI, 509 pages. 1981.

Vol. 191: H. R. Sneessens, Theory and Estimation of Macroeconomic Rationing Models. VII, 138 pages. 1981.

Vol. 192: H. J. Bierens: Robust Methods and Asymptotic Theory in Nonlinear Econometrics. IX, 198 pages. 1981.

Vol. 193: J. K. Sengupta, Optimal Decisions under Uncertainty. VII, 156 pages. 1981.

Vol. 194: R. W. Shephard, Cost and Production Functions. XI, 104 pages. 1981.

Vol. 195: H. W. Ursprung, Die elementare Katastrophentheorie. Eine Darstellung aus der Sicht der Ökonomie. VII, 332 pages. 1982.

Vol. 196: M. Nermuth, Information Structures in Economics. VIII, 236 pages. 1982.

Vol. 197: Integer Programming and Related Areas. A Classified Bibliography. 1978 – 1981. Edited by R. von Randow. XIV, 338 pages. 1982.

Vol. 198: P. Zweifel, Ein ökonomisches Modell des Arztverhaltens. XIX, 392 Seiten. 1982.

Vol. 199: Evaluating Mathematical Programming Techniques. Proceedings, 1981. Edited by J.M. Mulvey. XI, 379 pages. 1982.

Vol. 200: The Resource Sector in an Open Economy. Edited by H. Siebert. IX, 161 pages. 1984.

Vol. 201: P. M. C. de Boer, Price Effects in Input-Output-Relations: A Theoretical and Empirical Study for the Netherlands 1949–1967. X, 140 pages. 1982.

Vol. 202: U. Witt, J. Perske, SMS – A Program Package for Simulation and Gaming of Stochastic Market Processes and Learning Behavior. VII, 266 pages. 1982.

Vol. 203: Compilation of Input-Output Tables. Proceedings, 1981. Edited by J. V. Skolka. VII, 307 pages. 1982.

Vol. 204: K.C. Mosler, Entscheidungsregeln bei Risiko: Multivariate stochastische Dominanz. VII, 172 Seiten. 1982.

Vol. 205: R. Ramanathan, Introduction to the Theory of Economic Growth. IX, 347 pages. 1982.

Vol. 206: M.H. Karwan, V. Lotfi, J. Telgen, and S. Zionts, Redundancy in Mathematical Programming. VII, 286 pages. 1983.

Vol. 207: Y. Fujimori, Modern Analysis of Value Theory. X, 165 pages. 1982.

Vol. 208: Econometric Decision Models. Proceedings, 1981. Edited by J. Gruber. VI, 364 pages. 1983.

Vol. 209: Essays and Surveys on Multiple Criteria Decision Making. Proceedings, 1982. Edited by P. Hansen. VII, 441 pages. 1983.

Vol. 210: Technology, Organization and Economic Structure. Edited by R. Sato and M.J. Beckmann. VIII, 195 pages. 1983.

Vol. 211: P. van den Heuvel, The Stability of a Macroeconomic System with Quantity Constraints. VII, 169 pages. 1983.

Vol. 212: R. Sato and T. Nôno, Invariance Principles and the Structure of Technology. V, 94 pages. 1983.

Vol. 213: Aspiration Levels in Bargaining and Economic Decision Making. Proceedings, 1982. Edited by R. Tietz. VIII, 406 pages. 1983.

Vol. 214: M. Faber, H. Niemes und G. Stephan, Entropie, Umweltschutz und Rohstoffverbrauch. IX, 181 Seiten. 1983.

Vol. 215: Semi-Infinite Programming and Applications. Proceedings, 1981. Edited by A.V. Fiacco and K.O. Kortanek. XI, 322 pages. 1983.

Vol. 216: H.H. Müller, Fiscal Policies in a General Equilibrium Model with Persistent Unemployment. VI, 92 pages. 1983.

Vol. 217: Ch. Grootaert, The Relation Between Final Demand and Income Distribution. XIV, 105 pages. 1983.

Vol. 218: P. van Loon, A Dynamic Theory of the Firm: Production, Finance and Investment. VII, 191 pages. 1983.

Vol. 219: E. van Damme, Refinements of the Nash Equilibrium Concept. VI, 151 pages. 1983.

Vol. 220: M. Aoki, Notes on Economic Time Series Analysis: System Theoretic Perspectives. IX, 249 pages. 1983.

Vol. 221: S. Nakamura, An Inter-Industry Translog Model of Prices and Technical Change for the West German Economy. XIV, 290 pages. 1984.

Vol. 222: P. Meier, Energy Systems Analysis for Developing Countries. VI, 344 pages. 1984.

Vol. 223: W. Trockel, Market Demand. VIII, 205 pages. 1984.

Vol. 224: M. Kiy, Ein disaggregiertes Prognosesystem für die Bundesrepublik Deutschland. XVIII, 276 Seiten. 1984.

Vol. 225: T.R. von Ungern-Sternberg, Zur Analyse von Märkten mit unvollständiger Nachfragerinformation. IX, 125 Seiten. 1984

Vol. 226: Selected Topics in Operations Research and Mathematical Economics. Proceedings, 1983. Edited by G. Hammer and D. Pallaschke. IX, 478 pages. 1984.

Vol. 227: Risk and Capital. Proceedings, 1983. Edited by G. Bamberg and K. Spremann. VII, 306 pages. 1984.

Vol. 228: Nonlinear Models of Fluctuating Growth. Proceedings, 1983. Edited by R.M. Goodwin, M. Krüger and A. Vercelli. XVII, 277 pages. 1984.

Vol. 229: Interactive Decision Analysis. Proceedings, 1983. Edited by M. Grauer and A.P. Wierzbicki. VIII, 269 pages. 1984.

Vol. 230: Macro-Economic Planning with Conflicting Goals. Proceedings, 1982. Edited by M. Despontin, P. Nijkamp and J. Spronk. VI, 297 pages. 1984.

Vol. 231: G.F. Newell, The M/M/∞ Service System with Ranked Servers in Heavy Traffic. XI, 126 pages. 1984.

Vol. 232: L. Bauwens, Bayesian Full Information Analysis of Simultaneous Equation Models Using Integration by Monte Carlo. VI, 114 pages. 1984.

Vol. 233: G. Wagenhals, The World Copper Market. XI, 190 pages. 1984.

Vol. 234: B.C. Eaves, A Course in Triangulations for Solving Equations with Deformations. III, 302 pages. 1984.

Vol. 235: Stochastic Models in Reliability Theory. Proceedings, 1984. Edited by S. Osaki and Y. Hatoyama. VII, 212 pages. 1984.

Vol. 236: G. Gandolfo, P.C. Padoan, A Disequilibrium Model of Real and Financial Accumulation in an Open Economy. VI, 172 pages. 1984.

Vol. 237: Misspecification Analysis. Proceedings, 1983. Edited by T.K. Dijkstra. V, 129 pages. 1984.

Vol. 238: W. Domschke, A. Drexl, Location and Layout Planning. IV, 134 pages. 1985.

Vol. 239: Microeconomic Models of Housing Markets. Edited by K. Stahl. VII, 197 pages. 1985.

Vol. 240: Contributions to Operations Research. Proceedings, 1984. Edited by K. Neumann and D. Pallaschke. V, 190 pages. 1985.

Vol. 241: U. Wittmann, Das Konzept rationaler Preiserwartungen. XI, 310 Seiten. 1985.

Vol. 242: Decision Making with Multiple Objectives. Proceedings, 1984. Edited by Y. Y. Haimes and V. Chankong. XI, 571 pages. 1985.

Vol. 243: Integer Programming and Related Areas. A Classified Bibliography 1981–1984. Edited by R. von Randow. XX, 386 pages. 1985.

Vol. 244: Advances in Equilibrium Theory. Proceedings, 1984. Edited by C. D. Aliprantis, O. Burkinshaw and N. J. Rothman. II, 235 pages. 1985.

Vol. 245: J. E. M. Wilhelm, Arbitrage Theory. VII, 114 pages. 1985.

Vol. 246: P. W. Otter, Dynamic Feature Space Modelling, Filtering and Self-Tuning Control of Stochastic Systems. XIV, 177 pages. 1985.

Vol. 247: Optimization and Discrete Choice in Urban Systems. Proceedings, 1983. Edited by B. G. Hutchinson, P. Nijkamp and M. Batty. VI, 371 pages. 1985.

Vol. 248: Plural Rationality and Interactive Decision Processes. Proceedings, 1984. Edited by M. Grauer, M. Thompson and A.P. Wierzbicki. VI, 354 pages. 1985.

Vol. 249: Spatial Price Equilibrium: Advances in Theory, Computation and Application. Proceedings, 1984. Edited by P. T. Harker. VII, 277 pages. 1985.

Vol. 250: M. Roubens, Ph. Vincke, Preference Modelling. VIII, 94 pages. 1985.

Vol. 251: Input-Output Modeling. Proceedings, 1984. Edited by A. Smyshlyaev. VI, 261 pages. 1985.

Vol. 252: A. Birolini, On the Use of Stochastic Processes in Modeling Reliability Problems. VI, 105 pages. 1985.

Vol. 253: C. Withagen, Economic Theory and International Trade in Natural Exhaustible Resources. VI, 172 pages. 1985.

Vol. 254: S. Müller, Arbitrage Pricing of Contingent Claims. VIII, 151 pages. 1985.

Vol. 255: Nondifferentiable Optimization: Motivations and Applications. Proceedings, 1984. Edited by V.F. Demyanov and D. Pallaschke. VI, 350 pages. 1985.

Vol. 256: Convexity and Duality in Optimization. Proceedings, 1984. Edited by J. Ponstein. V, 142 pages. 1985.

Vol. 257: Dynamics of Macrosystems. Proceedings, 1984. Edited by J.-P. Aubin, D. Saari and K. Sigmund. VI, 280 pages. 1985.

Vol. 258: H. Funke, Eine allgemeine Theorie der Polypol- und Oligopolpreisbildung. III, 237 pages. 1985.

Vol. 259: Infinite Programming. Proceedings, 1984. Edited by E. J. Anderson and A. B. Philpott. XIV, 244 pages. 1985.

Vol. 260: H.-J. Kruse, Degeneracy Graphs and the Neighbourhood Problem. VIII, 128 pages. 1986.

Vol. 261: Th. R. Gulledge, Jr., N.K. Womer, The Economics of Made-to-Order Production. VI, 134 pages. 1986.

Vol. 262: H.U. Buhl, A Neo-Classical Theory of Distribution and Wealth. V, 146 pages. 1986.

Vol. 263: M. Schäfer, Resource Extraction and Market Structure. XI, 154 pages. 1986.

Vol. 264: Models of Economic Dynamics. Proceedings, 1983. Edited by H.F. Sonnenschein. VII, 212 pages. 1986.

Vol. 265: Dynamic Games and Applications in Economics. Edited by T. Başar. IX, 288 pages. 1986.

Vol. 266: Multi-Stage Production Planning and Inventory Control. Edited by S. Axsäter, Ch. Schneeweiss and E. Silver. V, 264 pages. 1986.

Vol. 267: R. Bemelmans, The Capacity Aspect of Inventories. IX, 165 pages. 1986.

Vol. 268: V. Firchau, Information Evaluation in Capital Markets. VII, 103 pages. 1986.

Vol. 269: A. Borglin, H. Keiding, Optimality in Infinite Horizon Economies. VI, 180 pages. 1986.

Vol. 270: Technological Change, Employment and Spatial Dynamics. Proceedings 1985. Edited by P. Nijkamp. VII, 466 pages. 1986.

Vol. 271: C. Hildreth, The Cowles Commission in Chicago, 1939–1955. V, 176 pages. 1986.

Vol. 272: G. Clemenz, Credit Markets with Asymmetric Information. VIII, 212 pages. 1986.

Vol. 273: Large-Scale Modelling and Interactive Decision Analysis. Proceedings, 1985. Edited by G. Fandel, M. Grauer, A. Kurzhanski and A. P. Wierzbicki. VII, 363 pages. 1986.

Vol. 274: W.K. Klein Haneveld, Duality in Stochastic Linear and Dynamic Programming. VII, 295 pages. 1986.

Vol. 275: Competition, Instability, and Nonlinear Cycles. Proceedings, 1985. Edited by W. Semmler. XII, 340 pages. 1986.

Vol. 276: M.R. Baye, D.A. Black, Consumer Behavior, Cost of Living Measures, and the Income Tax. VII, 119 pages. 1986.

Vol. 277: Studies in Austrian Capital Theory, Investment and Time. Edited by M. Faber. VI, 317 pages. 1986.

Vol. 278: W.E. Diewert, The Measurement of the Economic Benefits of Infrastructure Services. V, 202 pages. 1986.

Vol. 279: H.-J. Büttler, G. Frei and B. Schips, Estimation of Disequilibrium Models. VI, 114 pages. 1986.

Vol. 280: H.T. Lau, Combinatorial Heuristic Algorithms with FORTRAN. VII, 126 pages. 1986.